"MY"
GOD!

**WHO HE IS
WILL CHANGE
YOUR LIFE**

MY GOD!

WHO HE IS
WILL CHANGE
YOUR LIFE

JOHN MARSHALL

My God!
© 2006 by John Marshall

John Marshall Enterprises
PO Box 878
Pine Lake, Georgia 30072
(404) 316-5525
www.graceview.us
jdm@graceview.us

All rights reserved. No part of this book may be reproduced, stored in a retrieval system, or transmitted in any form or by any means without expressed written permission of the author.

All scripture quotations taken from the New American Standard Bible®, Copyright © 1960, 1962, 1963, 1968, 1971, 1972, 1973, 1975, 1977, 1995 by The Lockman Foundation. Used by permission. (www.Lockman.org)

ISBN 0-9740693-9-6
Printed in USA

Cover design and layout: Cathleen Kwas

DEDICATION

I dedicate this book to the God of Abraham. God tested Abraham to offer up his son, Isaac, as a burnt offering. Obediently, Abraham traversed the geographic and emotional terrain to the place of stretching forth his hand to slay his son. At that moment, God provided a propitiary sacrifice—a ram caught by the horns. After this encounter, God certified His promises to Abraham. Since there was no one greater to witness His unalterable decree and hold Him accountable to perform it, He swore by Himself (see Genesis 22:1-16, Hebrews 6:13-18). ***It is to that God, of whom there is no greater, that I dedicate this book.***

I dedicate this book to the God of Isaac. As Isaac traveled with his father, Abraham, to the place on the mountain to be sacrificed, he wondered out loud, "Where is the lamb for the burnt offering?" It must have been soothing to his ears when he heard his father say, "God will provide." Shortly thereafter, Isaac would come face to face with the reality that indeed God does provide (see Genesis 22:1-16). ***It is to that God who provides that I dedicate this book.***

I dedicate this book to the God of Jacob. At Bethel, God appeared to Jacob in a dream. Within that dream, God showed Isaac a ladder set on earth that reached to Heaven. Angels of God were ascending and descending upon that ladder. Through this experience, God acknowledged the angelic assistance that He provides for His people and foreshadowed Jesus, His Son, who is our access and avenue to Heaven (see Genesis 28:1-22, John 1:51, Hebrews 1:14). *It is to that God who helps us get to Heaven that I dedicate this book.*

I dedicate this book to the God of my father, Cleveland Marshall (1906-1998). God used Daddy to prepare me as a receptacle of His faith. Daddy communicated his understanding of God like this: "Son, if you do what is right, God will not let anyone harm you, and He will show you what it is that you need to know by the time that you need to know it." *It is to the God who informs His people that I dedicate this book.*

I dedicate this book to the God of my former neighbor and employer, Rozell Merriweather (1918-2004). I grew up next door to Mr. Merriweather, and on numerous occasions when I hitchhiked the one-mile ride with him to the corner store, God used him to plant in me seeds of the practical wisdom gathered from life's experiences. God provided Himself a lasting testimony through one of Mr. Merriweather's favorite sayings: "Keep on praying, children. The Lord will fix it, and any way He fix it is all right with me." *It is to the God who fixes it "all right" that I dedicate this book.*

I dedicate this book to the God of the giant prayer warrior, Noel Beckford (1919-2005). Through Brother Beckford, God nurtured to fruition spiritual passion in the lives of many people. Frequently during a sermon, a Bible study, or just a moment of spiritual reflection, Brother Beckford would just grin and say, **"My God!"** *It is to the God who makes us stand in awe at His majesty that I dedicate this book.*

ACKNOWLEDGMENT

I will always be grateful for the editorial assistance of Andrea Griggs, Adrianne Pless, and Denise Baker. Thanks to them, my ideas are now readable.

TABLE OF CONTENTS

Introduction 1

Chapter 1: The Concept of God 3

Chapter 2: The Creation of God 13

Chapter 3: The Name of God 21

Chapter 4: The Names for God 31

Chapter 5: The Son of God 41

Chapter 6: The Spirit of God 53

Chapter 7: The Bible of God: How We Got the Bible 67

Chapter 8: The Bible of God: The Inspiration of Scripture 77

Chapter 9: The Salvation of God 89

Chapter 10: The Church of God: The Universal Church 101

Chapter 11: The Church of God: The Local Church 111

Chapter 12: The Church of God: The Membership 123

Chapter 13: The Will of God 131

For the Record 145

INTRODUCTION

THE PROPHET ISAIAH SOUGHT TO PROVIDE DIVINE structure for human life when He said, "All your sons will be taught by the Lord" (Isaiah 54:13). Jesus Christ, an ardent student of Isaiah, sought to refocus human awareness when He recalled, "It is written in the prophets, 'And they shall all be taught of God.' Everyone who has heard and learned from the Father, comes to Me" (John 6:45).

Why do so many know so little about God? Very likely, we know so little because we have been taught very little about God. Even within the church, we are apt to study much methodology and terminology before theology. According to Jesus, it is the theology of God that brings us into the church, that is, our saved relationship with God.

On any given day, we are apt to hear more blatant reports against God than for God. Through television, over the internet, within print media, and even by way of personal conversation, spiritual warfare rages all around us. Therefore, those of us who are with God need to lift up our voices like a trumpet and sound the "mightiness" and the "mighty" works of God. The Israelites sang, "This is My God, and I will praise Him" when Jehovah parted the Red Sea for them (Exodus 15:2). We, too, need to project our synchronized voices until our echoes resonate throughout the universe, declaring, "My God." No doubt, if the Israelites had kept singing *this* song, they would never have had to sing *that* song (see Deuteronomy 32:1-43).

How different are we from the Athenians who erected an altar for their unknown god? They thought that God was far away and beyond knowing (see Acts 17:23). But rather, God is near to us, even as near as our present breath, for scripture declares, "He is not far from each one of us" (Acts 17:27). Maybe if we would personalize Him, calling Him, **"My God,"** as did the apostle Paul (see 1 Corinthians 1:4, 2 Corinthians 12:21, Philippians 1:3, 4:19), we could overcome the handicap.

Therefore, I commend to you **My God.** Hopefully, this will at least start the journey toward a more comprehensive understanding of who He is and what He has done. God has engineered the church, for which His Son, Christ Jesus, died. God is the bedrock of this organism. Through the church, God seeks to do a celestial work, "so that the manifold wisdom of God might now be made known through the church to the rulers and the authorities in the heavenly places" (Ephesians 3:10). Indeed, all who are members of the church are members because of **My God.** Let us travel the pathway to the church and see what golden nuggets of God we might discover along the way.

CHAPTER 1

THE CONCEPT OF GOD

MY GOD. The full essence of God exceeds the capacity of the most intellectual human mind. When our minds have been stretched beyond their limit, the full essence of God still lies light years away. Neither the greatest human mind nor the synergy of great human minds can fully fathom the true essence of God. The more we comprehend about God, the more we realize that His vastness lies beyond human comprehension. Therefore, some would ask, "Why try?" Although He and His ways are beyond the ability of any human to figure out, it benefits us to try.

Do you remember when as a child you imagined that you could stretch yourself taller? You stretched, measured, and stretched some more. This routine probably did not cause any growth, but it did help in that it allowed you to assume some responsibility for increasing your height. That in itself was a benefit. And, likewise, learning of God allows us to assume some responsibility for knowing Him better. The exercise itself may prove to be very valuable.

Do not think for a moment that God is playing "peek-a-boo" or "hide-and-seek" with the human mind. God wants us to know Him and of Him. God is near to us and our understanding (see Acts 17:24-31). Even Jesus, His Son, explains Him to us (see John 1:18). Really, it is God who pursues us through the understanding of Himself that He provides (see John 6:44-45).

WHO IS GOD?

God is that being of which no one or no thing greater can be conceived. God is superior or more perfect than all else. He is the being in which all authority and truth resides. Yet, there are some things that God has not revealed about Himself. The things that He has chosen not to reveal about Himself are not intellectually approachable and not able to be understood. He has, however, revealed some understandable things about Himself. We ought to attempt intellectually to accurately approach those understandable things that He has revealed about Himself. Yet, we should realize that those understandable things about God do exhaust our human mental capacity.

If I could give someone a single challenge in their personal pursuit to know God, I would engage in "double talk" by saying, "Prepare to understand what you may not ever come to understand, but keep trying until you do." All the while, God is pursuing us and giving us an understanding of Himself that we are not likely to comprehend fully.

Delivering the ten commandments to the Israelites, Moses reminded them that there was just one true God: "Hear, O Israel! The Lord is our God, the Lord is one!" (Deuteronomy 6:4). The one true God has revealed Himself as the eternal and self-existent one. The Lord Himself declared that before Him, beside Him, and without Him, there is no other God (see Isaiah 43:10-13). God Himself is exclusively God.

He who is eternal has always existed and will always exist. He who is self-existent depends upon no one other than Himself for His existence. The self-existent one came into existence by His own power and remains in existence by His own power. Therefore, God is infinite and sovereign to the universe. Because He is infinite, He is exceedingly immense and inexhaustible without limits. Because He is sovereign, He wields the greatest supreme authority. The prophet Isaiah was correct when he declared that the God of all power and all the power of God reigned supreme over all other and all else (see Isaiah 45:5-25).

WHERE IS GOD?

Where would we want a God like this to be? Or rather, where would we want to be in relation to a God like this? Would we want to be in a favorable relationship with Him, or would we prefer to be in an adversarial relationship with Him?

Imagine this. God is near to us. To the rambunctious bunch at Corinth, God reminded them that He was near enough to them to comfort them: "Blessed be the God and Father of our Lord Jesus Christ, the Father of mercies and God of all comfort, who comforts us in all our affliction so that we will be able to comfort those who are in any affliction with the comfort with which we ourselves are comforted by God" (2 Corinthians 1:3-4). Comfort literally means to stand beside and console or encourage. Whenever we are comforted, God is there standing beside us. Wherever we discover attitudes of compassion and actions of comfort, God is therein. God is everywhere that we discover His character being exposed. Not only is God beside us, but He is also ahead of us, drawing us to Himself.

Although we will never know all there is to know about God, we must work to make sure that what we know and believe is true of God. We need a healthy perspective of God. God is not just the God of our imagination, nor can we reduce Him to being just the God of our preference. Job and those who presented themselves as his friends discovered vibrant truths about God. In the midst of Job's trials, he struggled to maintain his spiritual integrity and proper perspective of God. Often, our predicament is similar.

When we are in a predicament, what is our perspective of God? If we dare to ask for a recommendation, I readily suggest that we should view God as the *God who limits our disturbance*. Job was disturbed (see Job chapters 1-2). God allowed satan to take Job's wealth but not his health (see Job 1:12). Later, God allowed satan to take Job's health but not his life (see Job 2:6). Certainly, a loss of health and wealth will create quite a disturbance. Whatever the amount of misery our trials cause, the magnitude of the trial and the misery caused could have been worse. And without God, it would have been worse.

I would suggest that we view God as the *God who listens to our discussion*. Job and his friends ignorantly discussed Job's predicament (see Job chapters 3-37). Although they were unlearned, God listened to their discussion nonetheless. They took turns spouting their ignorance. Eliphaz, the first friend, spoke (see Job 4:1-5:27). Bildad, the second friend, spoke (see Job 8:1-22). Zophar, the third friend, spoke (see Job 11:1-20). Intermingled among the friends' discussion, Job offered three complaints. Job seemed to be fine until his friends discussed his predicament with him (see Job 1:22). He complained that God was punishing him (see Job 6:4, 9:17). He complained that God would not hear him (see Job 3:1-4, 19:7, 30:20-21). He complained that God allowed the wicked to prosper (see Job 21:7). Patiently, God listened to all their empty chatter.

I recommend that we view God as the *God who leads in our deliverance*. God delivered Job (see Job chapters 38-42). God issued a first challenge to Job (see Job 38:1-40:2), and Job responded (see Job 40:3-5). God issued a second challenge to Job (see Job 40:6-41:34) and Job responded (see Job 42:1-6, 10-17).

Years ago, I received a speeding ticket that normally incurred a fine of $85. I discovered that the company for which I worked employed the traffic judge as their lawyer. Before the court date, I presented my ticket to him. He said, "Just come to court and I will take care of it." On my way to school, I stopped at the traffic court with only $5 in my pocket. When my case was called, in the presence of the entire courtroom, the judge asked me, "Do you have $15?"

I answered, "No."

He said, "Do you have $10?"

Again I said, "No."

He angrily blurted out, "I am trying to help you!" But he did not lower the fine again. I had to borrow $5 from a person in the audience in order to pay my fine. The judge could have cancelled the fine, and I thought he would, but he did not. Yet as bad as it was with the favor of the judge (a $10 fine), it would have been worse without his favor. Even when God does not perform as we prefer, without Him it would be worse.

The mercy of God does not give us what we deserve (death). Instead, the grace of God gives us more than we deserve (life), which helps us to maintain a healthy fellowship with God.

We lose our healthy perspective when we search for answers to our "why" questions, but we retain our healthy perspective when we find answers to our "who" questions. Very little healing resides in knowing why disruptive things happen. However, much healing resides in knowing who will walk through the valley of the shadow of death with us. Satan urges us to abandon God when we do not know the "why" of our failures." God urges us to abandon satan when we do not know the "why" of our successes (see Job 2:10). God opens seas (see Exodus 14:21), reveals mysteries (see Daniel 2:28), and rolls away stones (see Mark 16:3). Knowing God and whom He sends to stand by us is of utmost importance.

IS THERE REALLY A GOD?

Frequently people ask, "Is there really a God?" As intriguing as the answer may be, we really do not need answers. We need relationships. When relationships exist, answers become secondary. Through Jesus Christ, we can develop a meaningful relationship with God. Jesus thought it necessary to remind His disciples that He was exclusively the only way to the heavenly Father (see John 14:6). A better question is, "Do we really need a God?" Who would deny that Job needed a God who limited his disturbances, listened to his discussions, and led in his deliverance?

The human spirit continually hungers for fellowship with God. In every culture, human beings grasp for someone or something that extends beyond self. On our best day we refuse to be complete existentialists—those who believe that the sum total of life, its purpose, and meaning may be found within the individual himself. Therefore, from the most to the least civilized nation, human beings crave for someone who is greater than self.

All over the world, human beings devote themselves to causes, ideas, and/or systems that are beyond themselves. Human beings remain unfulfilled when not expressing allegiance to God. The psalmist declared that his soul pants and thirst for God, longing to appear in His presence (see Psalm 42:1-2). The Samaritans attempted to satisfy their craving for God. Because of their emptiness, Simon tricked the people, from the least to the greatest, into believing that he was of God (see Acts 8:9-11). We are no different than those he tricked. The human soul is never at peace until it finds something or someone that extends beyond self. ***Yes, we really do need God.***

God has further revealed Himself in the principles of relationship and association. Through the great commission, Jesus indicated the relationship and association of the Father, Son, and Holy Spirit (see Matthew 28:18-20, Luke 3:22). God interacts with His creation and creatures. For relationship, the Son is in the Father and the Father is in the Son (see John 10:38). For fellowship, the Son is with the Father and the Father is with the Son (see John 1:1-2). For authority, the Father is not from the Son, but the Son is from the Father (see John 6:35-38). For authority, the Holy Spirit is from the Father and the Son (see John 14:26). They always work cooperatively together. They never work separately or independently of each other.

THE IMAGE OF GOD

God created mankind in His own image (see Genesis 1:27). To be in the image and likeness of God is to have similarity and be a concrete representation of God. Yet, it does not mean that we possess some physical identifying attribute of God. God is spirit (see John 4:24). A spirit does not have flesh and bones (see Luke 24:39).

So, what exactly does it mean to be in the image and likeness of God? To have been created in the image and likeness of God means to have been created with the capacity to speak good words and perform good works. Let us walk the trail to this understanding. Jesus provides our best opportunity for understanding concepts of God. It is Jesus who explains God to us and for us. "No one has seen God at any time; the only begotten God who is in the bosom of the Father, He has explained Him" (John 1:18). The word *explained* is our English word *exegesis,* which literally means "to lead out." Therefore, Jesus leads God out from behind the curtain of invisibility into full view. That is why Jesus Himself is said to be "the image of the invisible God" (Colossians 1:15).

Jesus will explain the image of God for us. By listening to Jesus' conversation with Philip, we can learn about this image. When Philip asked to be shown the Father, Jesus said to him, "Have I been so long with you, and yet you have not come to know Me, Philip? He who has seen Me has seen the Father; how can you say, 'Show us the Father'?" (John 14:9). Jesus then proceeded to talk about the words that He spoke and the works that He did. Jesus is in the image of God. Yet, He wrapped His identity in His words and His works. His identity image was and is His words and His works.

Why combine words and works? From the beginning God did His works through His words. Time and time again, He said, "Let there be" and "There was" (Genesis 1:3, 6, 9, 11, 14, 20, 24, 26). Jesus did His works through His words. Jesus said to the demons that inhabited the man in the synagogue in Capernaum, "Come out of him" and they came out (Mark 1:25). He said to the wind of the sea of Galilee, "Be still" and the wind died down (Mark 4:39). God has created us in His image. He has created us to behave like He and His Son behave. He created us with the capacity to speak good words and perform good works through the speaking of good words. It is worthy of note that when the apostle Paul reminded believers of their new self, which is created in the likeness of God, he talked most about their speech (see Ephesians 4:24-32, Colossians 3:8-10).

Thought Provokers

1. Meditate upon this paradox: God is unfathomable in His essence, yet He is near to us and wants us to know Him.

2. How have you felt God pursuing you?

3. What has been your response? What will be your response as a result of reading this chapter?

✧ Chapter 2 ✦

THE CREATION OF GOD

MY GOD CREATED THIS UNIVERSE. HE CREATED LIVING and nonliving matter. The book of Genesis contains the history of the beginning of creation. After placing the universe in position, God began the next phase of creation by issuing "ten commandments." Ten times God commanded by speaking the words "Let there be" and similar phrases (see Genesis 1:3, 6, 9, 11, 14, 20, 24, 26, 28-29). He spoke the universe into existence.

Several thousand years later, Jesus Christ authenticated the biblical record of the history of creation. When some Pharisees questioned Him about marriage, He referred them to the order of marriage from creation (see Matthew 19:3-4, Mark 10:6, 13:19). Jesus knew about the creation because He participated in the creation. God created all things through Jesus and for Jesus (see Colossians 1:16-19).

The book of Genesis contains the history of the continuation of the creation. God continued the creation by issuing another "ten commandments." Ten times in Genesis chapter one, God said, "After their kind" (see verses 11-12, 21, 24-25). He spoke the continuation of the universe into existence.

According to the theory of evolution, there is no first cause uncaused, nor superintending intelligence, nor divine guidance of any kind that has caused the universe and its inhabitants to be as they are. All that exists does so because of a meandering, blind chance that has taken place over eons of time. The General Theory of Evolution or Organic Evolution states, "On the other hand, there is the theory that all the living forms in the world have risen from a single source, which itself came from an inorganic form. This theory can be called the General Theory of Evolution."[1]

"Evolution is a fully natural process, inherent in the physical properties of the universe, by which life arose in the first place and by which all living things, past or present, have since developed, divergently and progressively."[2]

The Special Theory of Evolution states, "Things can and do change, but those changes always take place within very narrow,

---

[1] *The Implications of Evolution*, by Dr. George A. Kerkut, Pergamon Press, London, 1960, p.157.

[2] "The World into Which Darwin Led Us," by Dr. George G. Simpson, *Science*, April 1, 1960, p. 969.

very restricted limits." Cross-breeding produces this kind of evolution. This kind of evolution is always restricted to the "kind" that produced it (see Genesis 1:11-12, 21, 24-25). There is no controversy over this theory of evolution. Both evolutionists and creationists accept this theory to be valid.

Life came only from life. "Then God said, 'Let the earth sprout vegetation, plants yielding seed, and fruit trees on the earth'" (Genesis 1:11a). Even now life comes only from "like" life, "bearing fruit after their kind with seed in them" (Genesis 1:11b). The fact that God created the universe kills evolution dead in its tracks. The fact that God continues the universe—and how He does that—seals the coffin of evolution. It is now time, once and for all, to bury the lie of the general theory of evolution.

The evidence overrules the objections to the proposition that God created the universe. The creation speaks volumes about God. The creation says that God is powerful. The created universe never needs repair. No wonder God aggressively interrogated Job (see Job 38:1-15). The creation of the materials of the universe demonstrates His power (see Acts 17:24). From where did the power to bring the universe into existence come? It came from God Himself! The creation of the immaterial of the universe demonstrates His power. God created condensation and evaporation (see Amos 5:8, 9:6), gravity (see Colossians 1:17), and even the concept of forgiveness (see Ephesians 4:32). Indeed, forgiveness is a novel idea.

The creation says that God is not only powerful, but also wise (see 1 Corinthians 2:6-9). The order of creation demonstrates His wisdom. First, God created plants and then animals. Animals needed plants for food. Yet, for pollination some plants needed animals (bees) to survive. A day could not have been millions of years; if so, plants would have become extinct without the animals needed for pollination.

The organism of creation demonstrates His wisdom. The organism of the family and its unity argues for the wisdom of God (see Ephesians 5:22-6:4). The organism of the church and its unity argues for the wisdom of God (see Ephesians 1:20-23, 2:12-22, 3:1-6, 5:32-33).

GOD—THE FIRST CAUSE

The Athenians believed in, named, and provided statues for the gods they had named. Just in case there existed a god of which they were unaware, they provided an extra statue designating it for the "unknown god." When the apostle Paul saw their ignorance, he proceeded to inform them of the one God who really was unknown to them (see Acts 17:22-31). He persuaded some; others he was not able to persuade (see Acts 17:32-34).

The existence of God has been placed on trial. Many have asked, "If God exists, then why do disease, disaster, and death continually devastate the innocent?" This question has caused many to doubt the existence of God.

We build all our life upon the foundation of probabilities. Probability is the ratio of occurrences to non-occurrences. Probability is the percentage of assurance that something will occur, but it always falls somewhere less than 100 percent of absolute certainty. Within the human realm, there are no 100-percent absolute certainties.

There is never a 100-percent absolute certainty that the airplane will safely reach its destination. However, there is a greater probability that it will than will not. Therefore, with confidence we make reservations, purchase our ticket, and board the plane, telling our loved ones, "I will call you when I get there." There is a greater probability that God exists than that He does not.

Who put this universe here? The sun, moon, and stars are included in the universe. The existence of the sun, moon, and stars forces us to proclaim, "Someone put them here!"

Someone caused the universe to exist. All that exists is caused by someone who existed prior to the existence of what was created. This forces us retrospectively to an "uncaused cause," raising the probability that God exists.

This is what historians call the "cosmological argument" for the existence of the universe. *Cosmo* means "world" and *logos* means "reason." Therefore, this argument puts forth a reason for the existence of the world (see Acts 17:24 Genesis 1:1-31).

Who put life here? Plants, animals, and human beings are alive. Living plants, animals, and human beings force us to proclaim, "Someone put life here!" Some living one has caused life to exist. All that lives is caused by someone who lived prior. This forces us retrospectively to acknowledge the existence of a living uncaused cause. Even if there was a big bang, I ask, "Who pulled the trigger?" Someone had to rig the trigger and then pull the trigger. Challenge those who disbelieve in the existence of God. Ask them, "Who put the universe here?" If they resort to the big-bang theory, ask them, "Who pulled the trigger?"

GOD—THE FIRST DESIGNER

Who put this universe here like this? The sun, moon, and stars are arranged according to design. When we observe the arranged design of the sun, moon, and stars, we are forced to proclaim, "Someone put them here like this!" Someone caused the universe to exist like this. Design requires a designer that existed prior to the time of the design. This forces us retrospectively to acknowledge the existence of an "uncaused-cause designer."

This is what historians call the "teleological argument." The cosmological argument looks at the universe and sees "cause," while the teleological argument looks at the universe and sees "design." That designed complexity of the universe forces us to proclaim, "Someone designed it like this" (see Genesis 1:11, 14-19, 21-30, Job 26:7-10, Psalm 104:19, 139:14, Isaiah 40:22, Amos 5:8, 9:6, Acts 17:26, 1 Corinthians 15:40-41).

Who put life here like this? The plants, animals, and human beings radiate intelligent design. Intelligent design forces us to proclaim, "Someone put them here like this!" Someone caused life to exist like this. All intelligent design is caused by a designer that existed prior to the existence of what was created. This forces us retrospectively to an uncaused-cause designer of life. Even if there was a big bang, I ask, "Who pointed it in the designed direction in which it fired?" Challenge those who disbelieve. Ask them, "Who put it (the universe) here like this?"

The rotating, revolving synchronization of the sun, moon, earth, and stars argues for intelligent design. The synchronization of the complexities of life argues for intelligent design. Intelligent design always argues for an intelligent designer.

The creation worldview sees God as the creator who, through supernatural processes, is responsible for the origin, sustaining, and governing of the universe and all that is within the universe. The creation worldview is the basis for Christianity.

For the creationist, there are absolutes. Therefore, there is an objective truth. Within this creationist worldview, the apostle Paul argued for objective truth (see Romans 1:18-19, 25, 28, 32).

From first to last in scripture, God reveals Himself as the one and only true God, beside whom there is no other (see Deuteronomy 6:5, Isaiah 43:10, James 2:19). What is important is that we readily confess all that scripture affirms about God. However, we do not need answers, for they do not help. We need a relationship with God; that is what helps!

Thought Provokers

1. Meditate upon this statement: "The book of Genesis contains the history of the creation, and the history of the continuation of the creation."

2. How would you respond to someone who advocates the theory of evolution? As a result of studying this chapter, how does that theory stand in relation to your own beliefs?

3. What is the creationist worldview? As a result of studying this chapter, how does that worldview stand in relation to your own beliefs?

✧ CHAPTER 3 ✦

THE NAME OF GOD

MY GOD, WHAT IS YOUR NAME? WHAT DOES YOUR NAME mean? What does it indicate about you? Have you ever considered the significance of your name? How deliberate was your name-choosing process? If you have children, how deliberate were you in choosing their names?

In the ancient Orient, a name carried more significance than it does now in the contemporary west. A name indicated one's authority, character, and/or reputation. A name referred to the very essence of the person. It did much more than just distinguish one person from another. Therefore, to use a person's name was to reflect upon the very essence of that person's authority, character, and/or reputation. A name was the very vehicle in which the essence of the person rode. Whenever someone knew another person's name, he or she also knew the essence of that person.

A name contains an audible expression of one's authority. In ancient times when someone called a person's name, they were calling upon his authority. As God prepared Moses to return to Egypt to negotiate the release of the Israelites, Moses asked for the name or authority in which he was to speak to Pharaoh. In response to his request, God informed Moses of His own authoritative name (see Exodus 3:13-15). A time later when God had not delivered the Israelites from Egypt, Moses chastised the name or authority of God (see Exodus 5:22-23).

Eventually, God delivered His people from Egyptian bondage. As a means of protective care, He sent an angel to guard their way as He brought them to the designated place. God's charge to His people reminded them to obey the angel because God had placed His name (authority) in that angel (see Exodus 23:20-23).

God put His name in an angel. By doing so, God gave the angel authority (power and permission) to guard the way for His people. His name indicated His authority.

A name contains an audible expression of one's character. When someone called a person's name, they were calling upon his character. Abraham's son, Isaac, fathered twin sons, Esau and Jacob. Why did they ever name the boy Jacob? The word *Jacob* means "supplanter." To supplant was to put something under the sole or foot of another in order to trick, trap, or trip him. It is interesting to note that when Esau, the first born, came forth from his mother's womb, his brother, Jacob, followed with his hand on his heel (see Genesis 25:24-26).

On more than one occasion, Jacob trapped his brother, Esau. First, he "strong armed" Esau into selling his birthright for a meal of lentil stew (see Genesis 25:28-34). On the second occasion, Jacob tricked his father into giving him the birthright blessing of the firstborn son that rightfully belonged to Esau (see Genesis 27:34-36). Truly, Jacob's character resonated within his name (see Hosea 12:2-3).

As God began to utilize Jacob in His overall plan of redemption, He changed his name from Jacob to Israel (see Genesis 32:24-28, 35:9-10). What a demonstrative way to indicate a change of character.

A name contains an audible expression of one's reputation. In ancient times, when someone called a person's name, they were calling upon his or her reputation. After Abram had reached his seventy-fifth birthday, God promised him that he would have a son (see Genesis 12:1-7). The name *Abram* meant "exalted father," but the name *Abraham* meant "father of many nations" (see Genesis 17:1-5). God did change Abram's name to Abraham, indicating the reputation to come. Abraham was more consistent with the reputation that he would later have. Indeed, he became the father of many nations. Sometimes the reputation is not only what has already been done in the past, but what will also be done in the future (see Genesis 48:14-16).

God renewed his promise to Abram and changed his name to Abraham when he was ninety-nine years old (see Genesis 17:1-5). Within three months, Sarah conceived, and by the time Abraham was 100 years old, Isaac was born. How would people know that

Abram's name had changed to Abraham? Abraham would have to tell them. When Abraham began introducing himself by his new name, which indicated his reputation, he accomplished in three months what he had not accomplished in twenty-four years.

When God anointed Solomon king over Israel, Solomon prayed and thanked God for showing kindness to his father, David. He recognized that he was an extension of his father.

Then Solomon said, "You have shown great lovingkindness to Your servant David my father, according as he walked before You in truth and righteousness and uprightness of heart toward You; and You have reserved for him this great lovingkindness, that You have given him a son to sit on his throne, as it is this day" (1 Kings 3:6).

God's reputation continues to live in the sons and the grandsons.

When we use the Lord's name, we should reflect upon His authority. When we pray, sing, or teach, we should always reflect upon the authority of the Lord. Therefore, we should always internalize the authority of the Lord when we do anything in His name.

When we need a person's authority, we ask for their signature. When we sign a check, we give authority for another to go to the bank and retrieve funds. With a signed check, another person can go to the bank and extract money in our name.

When we use the Lord's name, we should reflect upon His character. Therefore, when we pray, sing, or teach in the name of the Lord, we should reflect upon His character. We should always internalize His character when we do anything in the name of the Lord.

When we use the Lord's name, we should reflect upon His reputation. When we pray, sing, or teach in the name of the Lord, we should always reflect upon the reputation of the Lord. Therefore, we should always internalize the reputation of the Lord when we do anything in His name. We must be spiritual in how we use the name of the Lord. We must be careful to honor the name of the Lord.

Within the code of the ten commandments, Moses cautioned against taking the name of the Lord in vain. "You shall not take the name of the Lord your God in vain, for the Lord will not leave him unpunished who takes His name in vain" (Exodus 20:7). We must be spiritual in how we use the name of the Lord. God seriously punished His people when they violated His name. It was an inescapable punishment. He did not accept a plea bargain nor plead guilty to a lesser crime.

To use the name of the Lord in vain is to use His name falsely. God allowed His people to swear by His name. "You shall fear only the Lord your God; and you shall worship Him and swear by His name" (Deuteronomy 6:13). "You shall fear the Lord your God; you shall serve Him and cling to Him, and you shall swear by His name" (Deuteronomy 10:20). To swear was to bind oneself formally and unconditionally within an agreement.

Esau swore to Jacob when he sold his birthright for a meal of lentil stew. Esau formally entered into a binding agreement with Jacob (see Genesis 25:29-33). Joseph swore to his father, Israel, when he agreed to carry the bones of his father out of Egypt to be buried. Jacob formally entered into a binding agreement with Israel (see Genesis 47:27-31). When the period of mourning for the death of Israel had passed, Joseph reminded Pharaoh that he had sworn to his father to bury him in the land of Canaan (see Genesis 50:1-5).

Therefore, Pharaoh allowed Joseph to proceed to bury his father according to his sworn agreement (see verses 6-13). God Himself swore to Abraham to multiply his seed:

Then the angel of the Lord called to Abraham a second time from heaven, and said, "By Myself I have sworn, declares the Lord, because you have done this thing and have not withheld your son, your only son, indeed I will greatly bless you, and I will greatly multiply your seed as the stars of the heavens and as the sand which is on the seashore; and your seed shall possess the gate of their enemies. In your seed all the nations of the earth shall be blessed, because you have obeyed My voice" (Genesis 22:15-18).

The inspired New Testament commentary on God's behavior forces us to accept the fact that God swore. It also helps clarify what it meant to swear. When God swore, He formally entered into a binding agreement:

For when God made the promise to Abraham, since He could swear by no one greater, He swore by Himself, saying, "I will surely bless you and I will surely multiply you." And so, having patiently waited, he obtained the promise. For men swear by one greater than themselves, and with them an oath given as confirmation is an end of every dispute. In the same way God, desiring even more to show to the heirs of the promise the unchangeableness of His purpose, interposed with an oath, so that by two unchangeable things in which it is impossible for God to lie, we who have taken refuge would have strong encouragement to take hold of the hope set before us" (Hebrews 6:13-18).

God disallowed His people to swear falsely by His name. "You shall not swear falsely by My name, so as to profane the name of your God; I am the Lord" (Leviticus 19:12). God is the very essence of truth and the very essence of God is truth. Anything that is not of truth should have no association with God; therefore, God prohibited swearing falsely by His name. To make an agreement falsely (one that could not or should not be kept) in His name was to use His name in vain.

To use the name of the Lord in vain is to use His name frivolously. God allowed His people to use His name for things of qualitative substance. God allowed the Levites to serve Him and bless others in His name (see Deuteronomy 10:8, 18:5). God allowed prophets to speak His words in His name (see Deuteronomy 18:18-19). God even allowed the priests to settle disputes in His name (see Deuteronomy 21:5). God selected Solomon to replace David as king over all Israel. Solomon recognized his insufficiency to rule and lead God's people; therefore, he asked for wisdom (see 1 Kings 3:6-9). God provided him the wisdom to rule accurately. On one occasion Solomon settled a dispute between two women regarding which baby belonged to which woman (see 1 Kings 3:16-28). Serving, speaking, and settling disputes are qualitative and substantive experiences. We can use God's authority, character, and reputation to serve, speak, and settle disputes. It is fitting, because His name is His authority, character, and reputation in His presence (see Deuteronomy 12:5), in His protection (see Psalm 20:1), and in His prominence (see Psalm 111:9).

God involves Himself only with experiences that are substantive and qualitative. We can see this when we observe God's productions, The ark, tabernacle, and even the temple were quality productions. His deliverance of His people from Egypt as well as His protective care in the wilderness all are qualitative and substantive productions. As a matter of fact, His productions were of such extravagant nature they astounded even the minds of those other than His people. "Now Jethro, the priest of Midian, Moses' father-in-law, heard of all that God had done for Moses and for Israel His people, how the Lord had brought Israel out of Egypt" (Exodus 18:1). Therefore, whatever we do must be first class.

God did not allow His people to use His name for things not of qualitative substance. He did not want prophets speaking in His name when He had not authorized their words. He promised to punish with death those who claimed to speak in His name when indeed He had not authorized them (see Deuteronomy 18:20-22). The very essence of God is qualitative substance. Anything that is not of qualitative substance should have no association with God. Indeed, God prohibited the frivolous use of His name (authority, character, reputation) (see Psalm 127:1, Jeremiah 46:11, Malachi 3:14).

How many times during the day do we say, "Oh, God," or "Oh, my God"? For what purpose do we call His name? Are we using His name for qualitative substantive experiences, or are we just calling His name out of habit?

Why do we say, "God this, and God that" when we are talking about things of no substance? Remember, God never embraces emptiness. We may have even called on God to help us get in front

The Name of God

of the driver in the next lane. In those instances, rather than calling on the authority of God, it is preferable to follow the Department of Transportation driving regulations.

Remember that God's name is venerable; therefore when His name is violated, His name will be vindicated. "You shall not take the name of the Lord your God in vain, for the Lord will not leave him unpunished who takes His name in vain" (Deuteronomy 5:11). Serious consequences befall those who use the name of the Lord frivolously (see Acts 19:11-17).

We must be spiritual in how we use the name (authority, character, reputation) of the Lord. Why do we say, "God is my witness" when we are not presenting truth? Remember, God never endorses deceit. God's name is venerable. When God's name is violated, it will also be vindicated (see Deuteronomy 5:11).

God wants us to use His name (authority, character, reputation). However, He wants us to use His name only for things of truthful substance (see Acts 19:11-17). Use His name for true praise. Use His name for true proclamation. "God is my witness; so help me God."

Thought Provokers

1. As a result of reading this chapter, what have you learned about the name of God?

2. When have you used the Lord's name wrongly?

3. What did that say to those around you about the character of the Lord, His authority, and His reputation?

CHAPTER 4

THE NAMES FOR GOD

MY GOD HAS SEVERAL DIFFERENT ASPECTS OF HIS HOLY name (authority, character, and reputation). The Old Testament was written in Hebrew. There are many different Hebrew words that are translated into English simply as *God* and *Lord*. Therefore, there are several common names or designations for the different aspects of His authority, character, and/or reputation.

Often we can know someone for a long time, yet realize there are many things we do not know about that person. When we come to know more about the different aspects of that person, it enlightens our fellowship with him or her. So it is with God. Knowing His different names educates us about the different aspects of Him. That additional knowledge enriches our fellowship with Him. Therefore, when we pray, we should conceptualize various aspects of the name of the Lord.

The Hebrew word *Adonai* (which is #H136 in *Strong's Exhaustive Concordance of the Bible*) represents one aspect of the name of the Lord. The designation *Adonai* occurs some 300 times in the Old Testament and frequently is translated as *Lord*. *Adonai* proclaims divine authority and refers to God's administrative ownership of everything that existed. *Adonai* suggests lordship on the part of God and stewardship on the part of His people (see Exodus 4:10-13, Isaiah 6:1, 8, 11).

The Hebrew word *Elohim* (Strong's #H430) is a plural name for God. *Elohim* means "the great one who is to be revered because of who He is" (see Exodus 20:7, Deuteronomy 6:4, Psalm 100:3). It occurs more than 2,700 times in the Bible. It occurs thirty-two times in the first chapter of Genesis. The Bible opens with the assertion that *Elohim* is the creator (see Genesis 1:1-31). The prefix *El* was an ancient Hebrew prefix meaning God. *Elohim* expresses the might of the creator as the sustainer of this universe (see Genesis 1:1, Acts 17:24, Hebrews 3:4). *Elohim* is even the creator of natural laws such as laws of gravity, condensation and evaporation, and more (see Amos 5:8, 9:6, Isaiah 55:8-10, Jeremiah 10:13, 51:16).

The Hebrew word *El Shaddai* (Strong's #H410 for *El* and #H7706 for *Shaddai*) represents another aspect of the name of the Lord. *El* means "great and glorious God," and *Shaddai* means "almighty." The designation *El Shaddai* occurs forty-eight times in the Old Testament and is always translated as "almighty." In the Septuagint, which is the Greek translation of the Hebrew scripture, it is rendered a number of times by the Greek word for "all-sufficient." *El Shaddai* derives from a root word that means "the strong, powerful, and sufficient one" who nourishes and destroys. This describes the disciplinarian nature of God.

It is used in connection with a blessing that only a powerful God could fulfill. Only *El Shaddai*, the Almighty, could bless Abraham and Sarah with a son when they were 100 and ninety years old respectively (see Genesis 17:1-6, 35:11-12). It is used in connection with affliction and chastisement (see Ruth 1:20-21, Job 5:17, 6:4, Isaiah 13:6, Joel 1:15). Sometimes *Shaddai* occurs without the prefix *El*, as in the case of Jacob giving his last will and testimony to his sons (see Genesis 49:25).

Remember, we must think spiritually as we use the name (authority, character, and reputation) of God. We must be spiritual in how we use the name (authority, character, and reputation) of the Lord. God is *Adonai*, our administrator and ruler. God is *Elohim*, our creator. God is our *El Shaddai*, our Almighty. It is good to speak frequently the diverse names of our Lord.

The Hebrew word *Jehovah* or *Yahweh* is how God introduced Himself to Moses, and it means "lord." "God *[Elohim]* spoke further to Moses and said to him, 'I am the Lord *[Jehovah]*; and I appeared to Abraham, Isaac, and Jacob, as God Almighty *[El Shaddai]*, but by My name, Lord *[Yahweh]*, I did not make Myself known to them'" (Exodus 6:2-3). Abraham knew God from one aspect, but did not know Him as *Yahweh*. God revealed an aspect of Himself to Moses that He did not reveal to Abraham.

The Hebrews would often write leaving out the vowels of their words. Therefore, *Yahweh* was represented by the letters YHWH, YHVH and later JHVH, for the Hebrew alphabet contained no letter J until the 1600s.

Long before the birth of Jesus, the Jews stopped pronouncing this actual name. They believed that to speak the name of God was to take His name in vain. When they read the scriptures and came to "YHVH," they would say, "Adonai," the Hebrew word for *Lord*. Sometimes they would just say, "Lord." *Adonai* was sometimes spelled as *Edonai*. By refusing to pronounce the name, they had made the pronunciation of His name the object of His name. To them, the pronunciation of His name was more sacred than He who was named. How unfortunate that is.

After the 1600s when the letter J had come into existence, some English Bible translations removed the first three vowels E, O, and A from the word *Edonai* and placed them between the letters JHVH, resulting in the word *JeHoVaH*. Other English translations followed the spirit of the reverent Hebrews and translated the "sacred four" letters as "the Lord" (all capitals). The next time one of the "Watchtower Witnesses" engage us in a discussion arguing that *Jehovah* is the all-exclusive name for God, it is effective to ask them what was His exclusive name before the 1600s.

Jehovah (Strong's #H3068) is used more than 6,800 times within scripture. *Jehovah* was God's plain name; it just emphasized His substance. *Jehovah* is His all-purpose name and communicates the reality of His existence. It is derived from the verb translated "to be." All other names for God are derived from His works except *Jehovah*, which just announces unequivocally the substance or existence of God. No wonder then in His answer to Moses' question of His identity, God simply declared, "I AM WHO I AM" (Exodus 3:14).

COVENANT NAMES

Jehovah introduced Himself by several covenant names. His covenant names are presented as compound names. These covenant (compound) names provide tremendous diversity of understanding. We need to know *Jehovah's* covenant names.

Jehovah-Jireh (Strong's #H7200) means "the Lord will provide." This is the actual rendering of His name. "Abraham called the name of that place The Lord Will Provide, as it is said to this day, 'In the mount of the Lord it will be provided'" (Genesis 22:14). The word *provide* is of Latin descent. The prefix *pro* means "before," and the suffix *vide* means "to see." In this instance, God's name means "to see before." Indeed, He is the God who sees everything beforehand. God stood at the beginning of human history and saw that everything was provided for beforehand (see Genesis 22:1-14). Even before Abraham began to offer up his son as a sacrifice, God had already provided a ram to be offered.

Understanding this designation of God surely enriches our fellowship with Him. God is our provider because He sees beforehand and has already worked out the details. Nothing catches God off guard nor finds Him unprepared.

When the son, Isaac, asked, "Where is the lamb?" the father, Abraham, responded, "God will provide." With great confidence,

Abraham just walked on together with his son. What a marvelous demonstration of faith in the presence of a son. Parents need to know and understand that God is *Jehovah-Jireh*. When children ask, "Where is the money to pay the bills?" the fathers should answer, "Jehovah-Jireh." God has already seen before hand and has provided. Why does God provide? He provides because that is who He is.

Jesus taught that same principle when He warned His disciples against worrying. He told them that God knows what they need and has provided for their needs (see Matthew 6:25-34). Knowledge of *Jehovah-Jireh* underscores the truth that "there is no need to worry." What a powerful principle of spiritual convictions.

Jehovah-Rophe (Strong's #H7495) means to "heal, restore, and/or cure." This is the one covenant name that God gave for Himself, as we see in Exodus 15:22-26.

And He said, "If you will give earnest heed to the voice of the Lord your God, and do what is right in His sight, and give ear to His commandments, and keep all His statutes, I will put none of the diseases on you which I have put on the Egyptians; for I, the Lord, am your healer" (Exodus 15:26).

By His mighty hand, the Lord delivered the children of Israel out from the bondage of Pharaoh in Egypt. After they had crossed the Red Sea, they broke forth singing the first recorded song in the Bible (see verses 1-21). Praise permeated that piece of prose. What do we do when God parts an entire sea for us? We just praise His name. At each success point in life, it is good to compose a song. When God has performed His awesome feats, we ought to compose a song that honors Him, and then we should keep singing that song even throughout the next challenge.

Unfortunately, the Israelites sang only for a little while. Three days into the wilderness, they found no drinking water (see verses 22-26). Instead of singing the praises of God, they allowed their circumstances to dictate their attitude toward their leader, and they grumbled at Moses (see verse 24). They failed to reason that if *Yahweh* could hold back the walls of water in the Red Sea, at the very least He could provide drinking water. God demonstrated His healing power. He directed Moses to throw a tree into the water, and through that experience God provided drinking water (see verses 25-26).

Not only does God heal, but healing is who He is. God not only gives provisions of healing, but He gives us Himself, the healer. God promised to keep illnesses from His obedient people. We are not doomed by hereditary defectives. We are not cursed to suffer the hereditary organic deficiencies that have plagued our ancestors. Our family's biological DNA does not have to rule supreme. Often our behavior, more so than our genetics, causes our genetic predispositions to harm our health.

Jehovah-Nissi (Strong's #H3071 and #H5251) means "the Lord is my banner or standard." At Rephidim, the Israelites battled Amalek (see Exodus 17:8-15). While Moses' hands were lifted, Israel prevailed, but when his hands fell, Amalek prevailed. When Moses became unable to raise his own hands, Aaron and Hur stood on each side and kept his hands lifted. To remember this experience, God commanded Moses to write the record and recite it as a memorial.

In addition, Moses built an altar and named it *Jehovah-Nissi*, The Lord is My Banner (see verse 15).

Occasionally, groups of people would prepare a banner around which they would gather as a means of identity. The banner would be a visible representation of the power of God upon their life. The banner then became the standard to which and around which all the people of God must come. They understood that when they came to the banner, they came to the power of God. When they came to the banner, they came to the standard of God. God then became the banner or the standard for His people through which He brought blessings out of battles. The name *Jehovah-Nissi* indicates that God is our banner of identity and our flag of victory.

Jehovah-M'Kaddesh (Strong's #H6942) is used 700 times in the Old Testament. It means to "set apart for divine use." "You shall keep My statutes and practice them; I am the Lord who sanctifies you" (Leviticus 20:8). Through this name, God says, "I am the One who makes you holy." It follows the command to follow God's command (see Exodus 31:12-14, Leviticus 22:9-32). This name relates to God's sanctifying power. Even for Christians, sanctification is God's finished work.

Jehovah-Shalom (Strong's #H3073 and #H7965) includes the word *shalom*, and means "the Lord is peace" (see Judges 6:1-24). The word is also translated as "full, complete, finished, and/or perfect." Through the discipline of God, sin was purged and peace restored. God not only gives peace, but He is peace. God is the full, complete, and perfect peace that we all need.

Jehovah-Rohi (Strong's #H7462) includes the word *rohi*, which means "shepherd" (see Psalm 23:1-6). No other name invokes such tender and intimate touch as that of a shepherd (see Revelation 7:17).

Jehovah-Tsidkenu (Strong's #H3072 and #H6666). *Tsidek* means stiff or straight. It is translated as "righteousness." God becomes to us what He requires of us. God's righteousness is our standard.

"Behold, the days are coming," declares the Lord, "when I will raise up for David a righteous Branch; and He will reign as king and act wisely and do justice and righteousness in the land. In His days Judah will be saved, and Israel will dwell securely; and this is His name by which He will be called, 'The Lord our righteousness'" (Jeremiah 23:5-6).

Jehovah-Shammah (Strong's #H3074 and #H8033) means "the Lord is there." "The city shall be 18,000 cubits round about; and the name of the city from that day shall be, 'The Lord is there'" (Ezekiel 48:35). The people of God had become so desecrated that God had taken leave of His house. The presence of God means everything. God was coming back to His people. He now lives within us, His people (see 1 Corinthians 3:16, 2 Corinthians 6:16). Indeed, God is here.

Thought Provokers

1. Which of the names of God means something special to you during this point in your life?

2. Which of the names of God have meant something to you in the past?

3. Which of the names of God that you have read about in this chapter has shown you a different aspect of His character that you never knew before?

⁂ CHAPTER 5 ⁂

THE SON OF GOD

MY GOD HAS A SON, JESUS, WHO WAS CONCEIVED OF A virgin woman (see Matthew 1:18-23, Luke 1:26-35, Isaiah 7:14, Galatians 4:4). Because He was born of a woman, Jesus was endowed with the biological faculties of human nature. And because Jesus was conceived through the Holy Spirit, He was endowed with the spiritual faculties of divine nature (see John 1:1, Hebrews 1:8).

Jesus startled His friends and angered His enemies by referring to God as His Father (see Matthew 27:43). He took His own directions from God, pointed others to God, and depended on God for all His needs—including His resurrection victory over death (see John 5:19, 30, 17:3-4, Luke 23:46, Hebrews 5:7). At the same time, Jesus claimed a unique oneness with the Father (see John 14:8-11, 17:3-5, 20-23)—a claim that would be blasphemous were it not true (see

Matthew 26:63-65). Before leaving the earth, Jesus also promised to come again in the Spirit, and that through the indwelling Spirit, believers could enjoy intimate fellowship with both Him and His Father (see John 14:16-23).

WHAT IS GOD LIKE?

When we look at Jesus, we see what God is like. We need not try to understand God through human observation and logic, for Jesus, the only-begotten Son of God, has already revealed Him (see John 1:18).

Chapter one of the gospel of John lists several characteristics of Jesus. Jesus is the Word (see John 1:1, 14). Here, *Word* is translated from the Greek word *logos*. We obtain our English word *logo* from this Greek word *logos*. *Logos* (the word) was a visible demonstration of a concept. In other words, Jesus visibly demonstrated the concept of God. Hebrews 1:8 refers to Jesus as God.

In the beginning the Word existed. The Word was Jesus. The Word existed before He was born into the world as Jesus, the Son of God (see John 1:1). The Word was with God and also was God (see John 1:1). In the beginning, before the Word was born into the world as the Son of God and before there existed Father and Son, they existed as God. Long before anything else existed, they—God and the Word—existed as supreme beings who had always existed. Before anything else ever came into existence, there existed God and the Word. All things were made by the Word (see John 1:3). This fact is confirmed by Ephesians 3:9.

HIS LORDSHIP

Jesus is Lord (see Acts 2:36). As Lord, He is our course or point of continuation (see 1 Corinthians 8:4-6). In other words, through Jesus, God continually directs our life.

Also, scripture calls Jesus the "Wonderful Counselor, Mighty God, Eternal Father, Prince of Peace" (Isaiah 9:6). As the Wonderful Counselor, He counsels and admonishes (see Matthew 11:28-30, 18:1-6). As the Mighty God, He displays His strength (see Matthew 28:18, Colossians 1:13-18). As the Everlasting Father, His duration is eternal (see 1 Corinthians 15:20-26, Revelation 1:5-8). As the Prince of Peace, He reconciles (see Ephesians 1:2, 2:11-16). Yes, Jesus came to reconcile mankind back with God (see 2 Corinthians 5:18-19). The word *reconcile* expresses the concept of restoring peace. It means to "reestablish a favorable relationship or to change the judicial status from condemnation to justification."

We can be reconciled because of the birth of Jesus. We can be reconciled because of the blood of Jesus. The blood of Christ cleanses us from the guilt of sin *as* we are born into the family of God. We are redeemed by the blood of Jesus (see 1 Peter 1:17-23). To be redeemed is to have the ransomed price of sin paid by the blood of Jesus.

During the time of the law of Moses, the high priest continually offered animal blood as the sacrifice for sins. Now, however, by one offering of His blood, henceforth and forever more, Jesus has freed us from sin (see Hebrews 7:26-28, 9:6-14). By the blood of Jesus, we are freed from sin and situated into the Kingdom as priests (see Revelation 1:4-6). Never ask, "Can God forgive the sinner?"

The blood of Christ cleanses us from the guilt of sin *after* we are born into the family of God (see 1 John 1:5-2:1). An occasional sin does not necessarily indicate that one is not walking in the light. If so, for what is there to be forgiven? The "we haves" in 1 John 1:5-2:1 are in the present and durational tense, meaning we have continual forgiveness in the blood of Jesus. Because of what Jesus has done, we have forgiveness now and in the future. Never ask, "Will God forgive the saint?"

The blood of bulls and goats could never atone for sin. They merely pointed forward to the one who would come at the end of that age and put away sin by the sacrifice of Himself, namely Jesus Christ (see Hebrews 9:22-28). No sacrifice offered on the Jewish altar had ever taken away sin. After Jesus made atonement for our sins, He arose to be our eternal high priest (see Hebrews 10:12-14).

Jesus Christ did more than all the prophets, priests, and philosophers combined to improve the moral standard of the world (see John 7:45-46). Jesus was a dynamic, moral teacher (see Matthew 7:28-29)—but He was much more than just a great moral teacher.

HIS DEITY

God wanted people to know who Jesus was. Therefore He revealed to Peter that Jesus was His Son (see Matthew chapters 16-17). Jesus considered whom people believed Him to be of fundamental importance (see Matthew chapters 13-15).

Jesus argued that He was a divine being (see John 8:54-58, Exodus 3:14). The "I Am" meant the absolute timelessness and eternal existent one. Jesus exercised divine prerogatives (see Matthew 5:21-48). Through His "I say" passages, He exercised His claim to be the Son of God (see Mark 14:61-64).

Facts are stubborn things. They refuse to go away. Therefore, evidence for His claim demands a verdict. Who does the evidence demand that He is?

Option number one: Jesus is not the Son of God. Therefore, He is a liar and we can dismiss what He said and did. If Jesus is a liar, then two alternatives exist. If He is a liar, then maybe He did not know that He was not the Son of God. Therefore, He would be a deluded liar. If He is a liar, then maybe He did know that He was not the Son of God. Therefore He would be a deliberate liar. In either case, Jesus would be a liar. We could trust neither a deluded liar nor a deliberate liar.

Option number two: Jesus is the Son of God. Therefore, He is truth and we must consider what He said and did. If Jesus is truth, then two alternatives exist. We may accept Him. If we accept Him as truth, we can enjoy now and in the future the pleasurable consequences of our decision (see Matthew 25:31-40). Or, we may reject Him. If we reject Him as truth, we will endure now and in the future the painful consequences of our decision (see verses 41-46).

No other religious leader ever claimed to be the Son of God. No other claimed to be the only way to God (see John 14:6). Evidence for His claim demands a verdict (see John 20:30-31).

HIS RESURRECTION

God raised Jesus from the dead. By raising Jesus from the dead, God provided undeniable evidence. The resurrection of Jesus proves that Jesus is the Son of God (see Acts 17:30-32, Romans 1:4). The opened and emptied tomb is evidence for the resurrection of Jesus (see Luke 24:1-12, John 20:1-10). Who opened and emptied the tomb?

First, we consider the possible earthly force that may have opened and emptied the tomb. How likely did those who were favorable to Jesus open and empty the tomb? Those who were favorable to Jesus could not have (see Matthew 27:62-66). How likely did those who were unfavorable to Jesus open and empty the tomb? Those who were unfavorable to Jesus would not have (see Matthew 27:62-66, 28:11-15).

Second, we consider the probable heavenly force that may have opened and emptied the tomb. How likely did an angel roll away the stone? It is very likely that an angel rolled away the stone (see Mark 16:1-4, Matthew 28:1-7). How likely did God raise the body of Jesus? It is very likely that God raised the body of Jesus (see Mark 8:31, 9:31, Acts 2:24, 32).

The opened and emptied tomb is evidence for the resurrection of Jesus (see Luke 24:1-12, John 20:1-10). The resurrection proves that Jesus is the Son of God. The resurrection proves that Jesus is above Mohammed, Buddha, and every other false god.

The rapid and radical change in the understanding of the people is evidence for the resurrection of Jesus. First, let us consider the change in the understanding of the apostles, those who were favorable to Jesus. Through the ministry of the Holy Spirit, God changed the apostles (see John 14:25-26, 16:13). Their intellectual understanding changed. Before the resurrection, they were dull of understanding (see Matthew 16:5-12), but after the resurrection, they clearly understood how to respond appropriately in every situation (see Acts 2:12-14, 37-38, 4:7-13). Their emotional concept changed. Before they were convinced of the resurrection, they were fearful (see John 20:19), but after they were convinced of the resurrection, they were courageous (see Acts 3:13-31).

Second, let us consider the change in the understanding of the opponents, those who were unfavorable to Jesus. Through the message of the Holy Spirit, God changed the opponents (see Acts 2:40-41). Their intellectual understanding changed. Before they became convinced of the resurrection of Jesus, they resisted the implications of the prophecy (see Acts 3:11-26), but after they were convinced of the resurrection, they received the benefits of prophecy (see Acts 4:1-4). Their emotional understanding changed. Before they were convinced of the resurrection, their heart was closed (see Acts 2:23), but when they became convinced of the resurrection, their heart opened (see Acts 2:37-46).

The chief priests and Pharisees remembered that Jesus had promised to rise from the dead (see Matthew 27:62-63). They persuaded Pilate and he gave orders to secure the tomb (see Matthew 27:64-65). Therefore they sealed the tomb and placed guards outside to keep watch (see Matthew 27:66). In spite of all this, God resurrected Jesus from the dead. The empty tomb argued for His resurrection (see John 20:1-10). His post-crucifixion appearances testified of His resurrection (see John 20:19-21:14, 1 Corinthians 15:1-8).

The resurrection of Jesus provides proof for our faith (see Acts 17:31, Romans 1:1-4, 1 Corinthians 15:12-19). The resurrection assures us that God has fixed a day in which He will judge the world. To judge means to "divide, separate, or make a distinction or express a decision." God will divide, separate, or make a distinction and express that decision about the world. God has fixed the day, a point in time, when He will judge the world (see Romans 2:16, 1 Thessalonians 5:2).

The resurrection assures us that God has fixed a day in which He will judge the world in righteousness through Jesus Christ (see John 5:22). Righteousness is a condition of character that is acceptable with God. God will express His decision as to whose character is acceptable to Him. God will express His decision based upon whom Jesus has declared to be righteous.

For His apostles, Jesus Christ provided primary evidences of His resurrection. After rising from the dead, He appeared visibly, spoke audibly, and interacted physically with them. Using primary evidences, Jesus convinced His apostles that He had risen from the dead (see John 20:20, 26-27).

Jesus wants us to believe that He has risen from the dead. Yet, He withholds the primary evidences for His resurrection. He remains invisible, refuses to speak audibly, and stays beyond our physical reach. Therefore, without using primary evidences, Jesus intends to convince us of His resurrection. Using only secondary evidences, Jesus expects to convince us of His resurrection (see John 17:20-21, 20:29-31). For us, Jesus provides only secondary evidences.

Many people argue that secondary evidences of the resurrection of Jesus Christ are unacceptable. Yet, they readily accept secondary evidences for all their other beliefs. In fact, they substantiate most of their beliefs with secondary evidences. Primary evidences exist only within the generation that eye-witnessed the event. We have no primary evidences for the forming of the United States government. No primary evidences for the validity of the United States Constitution remain. Our judicial system bases all its convictions upon secondary evidences. Never have the convicting judge and jury eye-witnessed the crime, and usually they have neither seen the victim nor the original crime scene. Upon observing secondary evidences, which are the testimonies of others, they convict.

The proclamation of the apostles is evidence that Jesus has risen from the dead (see 1 Corinthians 15:1-7, Acts 2:22-36, 3:14-15, 17:30-31). The confirmation to the people is evidence that Jesus has risen from the dead (see Hebrews 2:3, Acts 2:37-47, 4:4, 17:32-34).

Christianity is not only a religion of ideas, but it also combines ideas with facts. Facts are subject to historical investigation. The teachings of Christ are important, but the heart of the Christian religion is not in what Christ said, but in what He did. His words of justification, redemption, and sanctification are characteristic words of Christianity that have their significance rooted deeply in His death on the cross.

Matthew ended his gospel with a bold declaration. He declared that King Jesus had been raised from the dead. The angel of the Lord initially convinced the women that Jesus was alive (see Matthew 28:8). The angel of the Lord convinced the women by what he said to them. He told them where Jesus was not (see Matthew 28:5-6a). The body of Jesus was not in the tomb. He told them where Jesus was (see Matthew 28:7). Jesus was on His way to Galilee.

The angel of the Lord convinced the women by what he showed them. He showed them what was in the text (see Matthew 12:40, 16:21, 27:63, 28:6b). The resurrection of Jesus had been predicted. The angel showed them what was not in the tomb (see Matthew 28:6c). The angel did not roll away the stone so that Jesus could come out, but so that we could look in.

The appearance of the Lord subsequently convinced the women that Jesus was alive. The appearance of the Lord confirmed what the angel had said to them. He corroborated the angel's message. He repeated what the angel had said to reduce their fear (see Matthew 28:5, 10). Also, He repeated what the angel had said to increase their faith (see Matthew 28:7, 10).

The appearance of the Lord confirmed what the angel had shown to them. His appearance confirmed what was in the text (see Matthew 12:40, 16:21, 27:63, 28:6b). His appearance confirmed that He was not in the tomb (see Matthew 28:6c).

The angel of the Lord and the appearance of the Lord argued favorably for the resurrection of Jesus (see Matthew 28:1-10). In spite of these credible evidences, many denied the resurrection of Jesus. In an attempt to substantiate their denial, they published a lie all over Jerusalem. Unfortunately, many believed the lie (see Matthew 28:11-15).

If the stories of Jesus are simply myths without historical basis, if He was not born of a virgin, if He performed no miracles, and if He was not raised from the dead, we would be of all men most pitied (see 1 Corinthians 15:19). However, the historical evidence that confirms the Christian faith is overwhelming. Even the uninspired ancient writings of first-century persons such as Josephus, Tacitus, Suetonius, and Pliny the Younger argue for the historical validity of Jesus.

Thought Provokers

1. What will you say when someone tells you, "Jesus was a good man, but He wasn't the Son of God"?

2. What will you say when someone tells you there is no primary evidence that Jesus is the Son of God?

3. What will you say when someone asks you for primary evidences for the faith in you?

CHAPTER 6

THE SPIRIT OF GOD

MY GOD IS FATHER, SON, AND HOLY SPIRIT. IN CONTRAST to what the scripture says about God and Christ, we are told little in detail about the Holy Spirit Himself. We may not know and understand all things about the Holy Spirit, but we ought to seek to know and understand all that we can know and understand about the Holy Spirit.

Scripture provides much information about the Father's qualities, purpose, loves, and role in salvation. It details even more about the Son volunteering to come and do the Father's will, His involvements in becoming a man, His earthly ministry, present activity, and imminent return. We do not, however, have this sort of detailed information about the Holy Spirit.

We read of the gospel of God (see Romans 1:1, 15:16, 2 Corinthians 11:7, 1 Thessalonians 2:2, 8-9, 1 Peter 4:17) and the gospel of Christ (see Romans 15:19, 1 Corinthians 9:12, 2 Corinthians 4:4, Philippians 1:27), yet we never read of the gospel of the Spirit.

Scripture repeatedly refers to holy men preaching Christ, but nowhere do we read of men preaching the Spirit. The Holy Spirit did not come to upstage the Savior (see John chapters 13-14). Scripture says that men of God preached the Kingdom (see Acts 8:12), repentance and forgiveness of sins (see Luke 24:47), and the cross of Christ (see 1 Corinthians 1:21-23). Never did men of God preach the Spirit. Such considerations arrest our attention when we hear so many prominent religious people proclaiming the Spirit, seemingly above Jesus.

The Holy Spirit was never the subject of their preaching, but rather He was the Worker who brought the preaching home to the heart, convicting and persuading men of the truth (see John 16:7-11). The indwelling of the Spirit is not an end within Himself. It is what He *does* that is the point. Uninformed people have made *receiving* the Spirit the point. The Word of God makes **what He does within our hearts** the point (see Romans 5:5).

Several hundred years before Jesus, God revealed that He was going to put His Spirit within the hearts of His people (see Ezekiel 36:27, 37:14). At that time, this was a revolutionary thought. Jesus made it clear when He said:

Now on the last day, the great day of the feast, Jesus stood and cried out, saying, "If anyone is thirsty, let him come to Me and drink. He who believes in Me, as the Scripture said, 'From his innermost being will flow rivers of living water." But this He spoke of the Spirit, whom those who believed in Him were to receive; for the Spirit was not yet given, because Jesus was not yet glorified (John 7:37-39).

Until Jesus was glorified, the Spirit could not be "given" as He is today. Neither Moses, nor the kings, nor even holy prophets of old had the Spirit like those who are in Christ. He did not indwell them as He does those who are in the Son.

God now gives the Holy Spirit to those who obey Him (see Acts 5:32, Romans 5:5, 1 Corinthians 6:19). Those who obey, namely our salvation obedience to the gospel (see Acts 2:38), receive the Holy Spirit. Jesus called it believing and being baptized (see Mark 16:16). Paul said, "Believe in the Lord Jesus" (Acts 16:31). Scripture says absolutely nothing about "praying a sinner's prayer," or "asking Jesus into their hearts." Jesus never said to do any of these things. The Holy Spirit is not promised to those who do them. He is given to those who obey the Lord, namely those who believe, repent, and become baptized (see Acts 2:38).

The Holy Spirit is the personal presence of God dwelling within us. God personally and powerfully dwells within all who belong to Him (see Romans 8:9, 1 Corinthians 3:16, 2 Corinthians 6:16). Therefore, His presence energizes our mortal bodies (see Romans 8:11). The Holy Spirit is the personal presence of Christ dwelling within us. Christ personally dwells within all who belong to Him (see Romans 8:9-10, Galatians 2:20, 4:6, Ephesians 3:17).

Jesus declared that the Holy Spirit would teach all things (see John 14:26). Therefore, the Holy Spirit exercises the power of revelation. He revealed to the apostles and prophets the message of scripture (see Ephesians 3:1-5). Also, He reveals the meaning of the message of scripture (see Ephesians 1:15-18, 2 Timothy 2:7, James 1:5).

THE APOSTOLIC GIFT OF THE HOLY SPIRIT

God gave His Spirit to His disciples. The Spirit provided various gifts for the disciples (see 1 Corinthians 12:4). For some disciples, the Holy Spirit provided the apostolic gift. The apostolic gift is a unique gift of the Spirit. The apostles possessed a unique and unequaled gift of the Holy Spirit.

The term *apostle* referred to one who had been commissioned, equipped, and sent with authority to represent another (see Matthew 10:1-4, Luke 9:1-2). Jesus personally sent those who would be His apostles (see Acts 1:1-3, 9:1-16). The apostles possessed this unique gift of the Spirit. Their gift of the Spirit was unique and unequaled. Therefore, their power and prerogatives extended beyond that of other disciples. Every disciple was not an apostle and did not speak in "other tongues" (see 1 Corinthians 12:28-30).

The Holy Spirit enabled the apostles to (1) perform signs that only they could perform, (2) distinguish themselves from false apostles (see Revelation 2:2), and (3) lay their hands upon other disciples and empower them to perform miracles (see Acts 8:18). A sign was (1) a supranormal demonstration of power, (2) a kind of miracle that had a purpose outside of itself, and (3) a miracle that led to something else. A sign's greater value was not for what it was, but for what it indicated. For the sign to benefit, it had to indicate something of value.

On the day of Pentecost, 3,000 believers received the gift of the Holy Spirit (see Acts 2:38-41), yet there exists no mention of anyone on that day other than the twelve apostles performing miracles (see Acts 2:43). On another occasion, some disciples were filled with the Holy Spirit, yet they never performed miracles until after the apostles had "laid hands upon them" (Acts 6:6).

THE ASSISTING GIFT OF THE HOLY SPIRIT

The assisting gift is a utilitarian gift of the Spirit. It served a definite utilitarian function. It was utilitarian in that it equipped disciples to perform specific functions. God gave it to help in the performing of some specific thing needed at the time (see 1 Corinthians 12:4-11). This gift was neither a sign of nor a reward for advanced spiritual attainment. The disciples at Corinth possessed this gift, yet they exhibited evidence of very low spiritual advancement (see 1 Corinthians 3:1-3).

The apostle Paul planted the church at Philippi (see Acts 16:11-15). Shortly afterwards, he left the area (see Acts 16:16-40). How would this infant church survive and nourish itself spiritually? The assisting gift of the Holy Spirit enabled it and others like it to survive.

An infant church needs information. Through the assisting gift of the Spirit, God provided information. During the infant years of the first-century church, the disciples had access to few, if any, written New Testament documents, for few had been written. Therefore, the apostles transmitted to the disciples the gift of knowledge. Through their gift of knowledge, certain disciples received information and disbursed it to all other disciples (see 1 Corinthians 12:8, Ephesians 3:1-5, Acts 19:5-6). An infant church needed confirmation. Through the assisting gift of the Spirit, God provided confirmation. During the infant years of the first-century church, the disciples had little knowledge of who were indeed true teachers of the Word. The apostles transmitted to the disciples the gift of power or signs. Through their gift of confirmation, certain disciples certified their credibility (see Revelation 2:2, Hebrews 2:1-4, Acts 8:5-12, 9:10-26).

An infant church needed administration. Through the assisting gift of the Spirit, God provided administration. During the infant years of the church, the disciples needed to perform tasks of leadership for which they were not equipped. The apostles transmitted to the disciples the gift of service. Through their gift of administration, certain disciples could provide administrative leadership (see 1 Corinthians 12:28, Acts 13:2-4).

We now have access to all the written New Testament documents; therefore, we can validate our information, confirmation, and principles of administration with principles from scripture (see 2 Timothy 3:16-17, Ephesians 3:1-6).

THE ABIDING GIFT OF THE HOLY SPIRIT

The abiding gift of the Holy Spirit is a universal gift of the Spirit. It was universal in that it was promised to all and was provided for all who obeyed the Lord (see Acts 2:38-39, 5:32). This indwelling presence of the Holy Spirit bears witness with our spirit that we indeed are children of God (see Romans 8:16, 1 Corinthians 3:16, Galatians 4:4-6). The abiding gift of the Holy Spirit functions before, during, and after our conversion. After our conversion, the Holy Spirit continues to energize us (see Ephesians 3:20).

This gift of God works with the power of the Word. God dwells in us (see 2 Corinthians 6:16, 1 John 4:12-16). Christ dwells in us (see Romans 8:9-10, Ephesians 3:17). The abiding gift of the Spirit is forever with the disciples, for He seals us (see Ephesians 1:13), energizes us (see Ephesians 3:16-20), and fills us (see Ephesians 5:18).

When we hear, believe, repent, and become baptized, God forgives and gives us His Holy Spirit. "Repent, and each of you be baptized in the name of Jesus Christ for the forgiveness of your sins; and you will receive the gift of the Holy Spirit" (Acts 2:38). Again, scripture says, "And we are witnesses of these things; and so is the Holy Spirit, whom God has given to those who obey Him" (Acts 5:32). Further, scripture says, "However, you are not in the flesh but in the Spirit, if indeed the Spirit of God dwells in you. But if anyone does not have the Spirit of Christ, he does not belong to Him...The Spirit Himself testifies with our spirit that we are children of God" (Romans 8:9, 16).

In addition to *giving* us His Holy Spirit, God commands us to be *filled* with His Holy Spirit. "And do not get drunk with wine, for that is dissipation, but be filled with the Spirit" (Ephesians 5:18). To be given the Holy Spirit is different from being filled with the Holy Spirit. God just gives the Holy Spirit. Giving (receiving) the Holy Spirit is not something we do, but something that God does. Being filled with the Holy Spirit is something that we do.

To be filled means to "fill up, cause to abound, furnish or supply liberally, to flood, to diffuse throughout, soak, or saturate." John used the same word to describe how the odor saturated the atmosphere of the house. "Mary then took a pound of very costly perfume of pure nard, and anointed the feet of Jesus and wiped His feet with her hair; and the house was filled with the fragrance of the perfume" (John 12:3). Indeed, that is exactly what happened to the house; it was diffused, soaked, and saturated with the odor.

To be filled with the Spirit is not equivalent to "a baptism of the Holy Spirit." We are never commanded to desire or seek a baptism by the Holy Spirit. That idea is foreign to scripture. Unfortunately, however, many await such an experience.

The phrase *be filled* was translated from the Greek verb *plerousthe* that was in the imperative mood. This means that it is a command. For example, the statement "Close the door" is in the imperative mood. Since it is not optional, we must study to understand its meanings, so that we may obey it. *Plerousthe* was also in the present tense. This meant that it commands continuous or repeated action. An alternate translation could have been, "Be constantly or continuously filled with the Spirit."

Did that mean that more Spirit is to be received? No! For example, Mary brought one pound of ointment into the house. One second after she had opened the ointment, the odor began to fill the house—yet there was a period of time before the odor had completely filled the house. That "filling" of the house did not mean that more odor was added within the house, but that the odor had expressed itself more completely throughout the house.

Also, *plerousthe* was in the passive voice. This meant that the subject was acted upon. For example, the house did not fill itself with the fragrance, but the fragrance filled the house. Therefore, the command "be filled with the Spirit" meant to allow the Spirit to fill up, to furnish, and supply liberally. It meant to flood, to diffuse throughout, and soak or saturate. When the Spirit saturates our mind, it also dominates and controls it. Being filled with the Spirit means to experience a moment-by-moment empowering of the Spirit. This empowering will equip us to conquer the daily challenges of life. The apostle Paul contrasted the result of being filled with wine with being filled with the Spirit. The alcohol of the wine paralyzes our center of inhibitions. We then do what we otherwise would not do.

When we are filled with the Spirit, He paralyzes our carnal center of inhibitions and seeks to substitute a spiritual center of inhibitions for us. We then do good that we otherwise would never do, such as forgive (see Ephesians 4:32).

We must not only think correctly, but we must think completely. How we think determines how we will behave. Therefore, incomplete thoughts produce incomplete behavior. Our thoughts must include all that the scripture says about being filled with the Holy Spirit. *How likely have we excluded some of what the scripture says about being filled with the Holy Spirit?*

Spirit-filled people respond appropriately toward the Lord. Spirit-filled disciples sing to the Lord (see Ephesians 5:19). Singing impacts our heart emotionally; therefore, we sing, making melody in our hearts. The word *melody* literally means "to touch the chords or strings of" the heart.

We who are Spirit-filled thank the Lord for all things (see Ephesians 5:20). Thanking God elevates and enlarges our concept of experiencing His favor (see 2 Corinthians 1:3-4, Hebrews 13:5-6). Too often we magnify the calamities without emphasizing the goodness of God. Some will ask, "If God is so good, then why is so much evil done." I ask, "If God is so bad, then why is there so much good done in the world."

Spirit-filled people respond appropriately toward family. The Spirit-filled wife respects her husband (see Ephesians 5:33). She demonstrates her respect by submitting herself (arranging in an orderly fashion under the guidance of another) to her husband (see Ephesians 5:22). Submitting is a voluntary arranging of oneself. It is what the wife does toward her husband, not what the husband has the wife do. A wife submits to her husband because Jesus is her Lord (see Ephesians 5:21-24). Also, she submits to her husband because he is head (see Ephesians 5:22-24). Submission within the family unity is both efficient and effective. A Spirit-filled wife can and will submit to her husband.

A Spirit-filled husband loves his wife (see Ephesians 5:25-33). Love is an attitude and an action caused by a need, but controlled by relationship and resources. A wife needs to be nourished and cherished. *To nourish* is to "promote health and strength." *To cherish* is to "provide warmth and affection." A Spirit-filled husband will nourish and cherish his wife.

Spirit-filled children obey and honor their parents (see Ephesians 6:1-3). *To obey* means to "hear and submit to the command as one being under authority." Children should obey their parents in the Lord, and with the quality of obedience as if they were responding to the Lord, for indeed they are. Parental obedience is foundational within nature. Even wild animals obey parents.

Spirit-filled children of every age honor their parents. *To honor* means to "assign the proper value and respond according to that value." We must first realize the value of our parents. We honor our parents with our lips and our labor. What we say to our parents and do toward them either honors or dishonors.

A Spirit-filled father educates his children. The Holy Spirit prohibited the father from exasperating his children (see Ephesians 6:4). *To exasperate* literally means to "anger for the purpose of anger." A Spirit-filled father will bring up his children in the training and instruction of the Lord. He will educate them in all things, all the way to maturity. This training consists of verbal explanations and visible demonstrations that entice correct behavior (see Exodus 12:21-26).

Spirit-filled people put on the whole armor of God and stand against satan (see Ephesians 6:10-17). To be filled with the Holy Spirit does not require one to speak in *unknown* tongues. John the Baptist was filled with the Holy Spirit (see Luke 1:15), yet he performed no signs (see John 10:41). Tongues were for a sign (see 1 Corinthians 14:22). *One can be filled with the Spirit and never speak in an unknown tongue!*

The Holy Spirit is the presence and power of God manifested toward humankind. Through the fellowship of the Spirit, believers within the believing community enjoy ongoing appropriations of love and grace. The mission of the Holy Spirit is to incorporate humanity into the body of Christ, for He baptizes all believers into one body (see 1 Corinthians 12:13) and enables us to live in Christ (see Ephesians 3:20). Indeed, the believer lives by the power of the Holy Spirit living within him.

Neither the Old nor the New Testament writers defined, described, nor precisely identified the Spirit. However, Jesus provided valuable insight. He stated that:

1. The Spirit proceeded from the Father (see John 15:26).
2. The Father (God) would send the Spirit (see John 14:26).
3. He (Jesus) would send the Spirit (see John 15:26).
4. The Father would send the Spirit at Jesus' request (see John 14:16-17).
5. The Father would send the Spirit in His (Jesus') name (see John 14:26).
6. The Spirit would abide in the disciples (see John 14:17).
7. The Spirit would abide with the disciples forever (see John 14:16-17).
8. The Spirit was to be a comforter, counselor, and helper (see John 14:26), literally meaning "one called alongside." Another translation is "advocate" (see 1 John 2:1).
9. The Spirit would teach the disciples all things (see John 14:26).

THE SPIRIT OF GOD

10. The Spirit would bring to the disciples' remembrance all things that Jesus had said (see John 14:26).
11. The Spirit would not initiate a message, but would teach what He had heard (see John 16:13).
12. The Spirit came not to be an innovator, originator, or imitator. The Holy Spirit's role is to call attention to Christ (see John 16:13-15).
13. The Spirit would bear witness of Jesus (see John 15:26).
14. The Spirit would glorify Jesus (see John 16:14).

Thought Provokers

1. How has this chapter changed your understanding of the Holy Spirit?

2. How has this chapter changed your understanding about receiving and being filled with the Holy Spirit?

3. As you read the descriptions of how people act who have been filled with the Holy Spirit, where do you see yourself? Where would you like to see yourself? Will you ask the Holy Spirit to fill you and help you?

✧ CHAPTER 7 ✧

THE BIBLE OF GOD: HOW WE GOT THE BIBLE

MY GOD GAVE US HIS WORD, THE BIBLE. HUMAN WISDOM did not produce scripture. Before scripture could come *from* the biblical writers (authors), scripture had to come first *to* the biblical writers. First, the word came to Jeremiah and then it went forth from him (see Jeremiah 36:1-32).

Through the Holy Spirit, God gave divine competence to those men who authored scripture. By His spirit, God moved them along the path of knowledge (see 2 Peter 1:19-21). His divine competence enabled them to express adequately the matters that God wanted to communicate. This process of inspiration resulted in a presentation to us of the wisdom of God conveyed through human shareable symbols (words).

Over a period of about 1,600 years, some forty different writers recorded the Bible. These writers came from various cultural and educational backgrounds. The first original handwritten copy of each book of the Bible was called an "autograph copy." The autograph copy of each Old Testament book was written in the Hebrew language. From these autograph copies, scribes made additional copies in the Hebrew language and circulated them among the people. These additional copies made by the scribes were called "manuscript copies."

In the second century BC, these manuscript copies were translated into the Greek language. That translation of the Old Testament scripture into the Greek language was called the "Septuagint." Jesus quoted from it and even referred to its divisions (see Matthew 22:32, Luke 24:44). The autograph copies of the New Testament books were written in the Greek language. Scribes copied numerous manuscripts and circulated them among the people. Some 5,000 manuscripts have been discovered in different places throughout the East.

The manuscripts of the earlier scripture (Old Testament) and later scripture (New Testament) have been diligently compared and translated into the English language. Basically, two types of translations exist: the "dynamic equivalence" and "formal equivalence." The dynamic equivalence is a translation of the exact thought, while the formal equivalence is a translation of the exact word. The New International Version is a dynamic equivalence. The New American Standard Version and the King James Version are formal equivalence. Scholarly translations do exist. *The Bible is reliable.*

If the earlier scripture (Old Testament) had never been translated from the Hebrew language, and the later scripture (New Testament) had never been translated from the Greek language into the English language, could we read the Bible? If the Bible had never been translated, we would need to learn both the Hebrew and Greek languages before we could study it. Thank God for reliable translations, for they greatly assist our study of God's Word.

About 1228, Stephen Langton divided the Bible into chapters. John Wycliffe initiated the first English translation of the Bible, and John Purvey completed it in 1388. In about 1448, R. Nathan divided the earlier scripture into verses, and in 1551 Robert Stephanus divided the later scripture into verses.

In Great Britain, between 1604 and 1611, during the reign of King James, fifty-four Bible scholars translated the Bible, calling their translation the King James Version—not because King James decided what the resulting translation would be, but simply because it was translated during his reign and at his encouragement.

Initially, the authors wrote the Bible to embrace the culture of human beings who lived on three different continents. It embraced the culture of the human beings who lived upon the continents of Africa, Asia, and Europe. For example, the eunuch was from Ethiopia on the continent of Africa (see Acts 8:27). The disciples who engaged in the dispute were from Jerusalem on the continent of Asia (see Acts 15:1-4). The apostle Paul left Athens and went to Corinth, which are both on the continent of Europe (see Acts 18:1).

In spite of being initially addressed to only three different continents, the scripture relates and applies to all human beings over the entire world. No Bible writer ever disputed what another writer had written. In spite of its diversities, the Bible uniformly describes: (1) the personality and character of God (see Exodus 34:6, Romans 2:4), (2) the personality and character of humankind (see Jeremiah 17:9, Romans 1:21-32), (3) the human need for forgiveness and salvation (see Exodus 32:32, Matthew 6:12-15, Luke 5:21-24), and (4) the anticipation and coming of a savior (see Deuteronomy 18:15-19, Acts 3:22-23). Without divine revelation, the human mind was and is incapable of producing the Bible.

THE TWO TESTAMENTS

The Bible is divided into two "testaments." The first testament is the Old Testament or the "earlier scripture." It contains thirty-nine books. These books are not arranged in chronological order. The Old Testament contains five books of Law, often called the Pentateuch: Genesis, Exodus, Leviticus, Numbers, and Deuteronomy. Laws are generally written in exact terminology with little or no symbolic and figurative language. We can expect the language of these five books to be exact and specific. For example, observe the exactness: "tenth day" and "fourteenth day" (Exodus 12:3, 6).

It contains twelve books of history: Joshua, Judges, Ruth, 1 Samuel, 2 Samuel, 1 Kings, 2 Kings, 1 Chronicles, 2 Chronicles, Ezra, Nehemiah, and Esther. These books contain a historical record of the wilderness wandering and promise land dwelling of the Israelites.

It contains five books of wisdom literature often called poetry: Job, Psalms, Proverbs, Ecclesiastes, and Song of Solomon. Poetry is usually written in highly figurative and symbolic language. We can expect these books to contain a lot of figurative language. For example, observe the figurativeness: "paths of righteousness" and "shadow of death" (Psalm 23:3-4).

It contains seventeen books of prophecy. Books of prophecy "foretold" or predicted future events, such as, "It will come about after this" (Joel 2:28). Also, books of prophecy "forthtold" or explained the predicted events once they began to occur. "But this is what was spoken of through the prophet Joel" (Acts 2:16). The prophecy in Joel "foretells" what the prophecy in Acts "forthtells." Five of the prophecy books are called the "major prophets": Isaiah, Jeremiah, Lamentations, Ezekiel, and Daniel. These are called "major" simply because of their long length, not because of importance. Twelve of the prophecy books are called the "minor prophets": Hosea, Joel, Amos, Obadiah, Jonah, Micah, Nahum, Habakkuk, Zephaniah, Haggai, Zechariah, and Malachi. These are called "minor" simply because of their short length, not because of lack of importance.

The second testament is the New Testament or the "later scripture." It contains twenty-seven books. These books are neither arranged in chronological order nor order of importance. Sometimes they are arranged according to length.

The New Testament contains four gospels, which are historical narratives of the earthly life of Jesus Christ: Matthew, Mark, Luke, and John. These books contain information from the time shortly before the birth of Jesus until shortly after His death.

The New Testament contains one book of history, Acts, which is the historical narrative of where and how Christianity began and grew. This book contains messages preached directly to and for those who had not become disciples of Christ.

The New Testament contains twenty-one letters. Nine letters were written to churches: Romans, 1 Corinthians, 2 Corinthians, Galatians, Ephesians, Philippians, Colossians, 1 Thessalonians, and 2 Thessalonians. Twelve letters were written to individuals: 1 Timothy, 2 Timothy, Titus, Philemon, Hebrews, James, 1 Peter, 2 Peter, 1 John, 2 John, 3 John, and Jude. Romans through Thessalonians were named for the city where the church was located. 1 Timothy through Philemon bear the name of the person to whom the letter was addressed. James through Jude bear the name of the one who wrote the letter.

The New Testament concludes with one book of prophecy: Revelation.

THREE DISPENSATIONS

The Bible is divided by time into three dispensations. A dispensation is a period of time when a particular system of revealed commands regulates human affairs. Throughout history, there have been three different dispensations or periods of time when God used a different system to regulate human affairs.

God has responded differently toward humankind in different generations (see Genesis 9:12-15). God's first period was the "Patriarchal Dispensation." It began with the dawn of creation (see Genesis 1:28-31). During this time, God made a covenant with the descendants of such patriarchs as Adam, Noah, and Abraham and their descendants (see Genesis 6:18, 9:9-17, 15:18, 17:2). In this dispensation, God communicated verbally with a leading male in each family called a "patriarch," for He had not yet produced written communication to govern humankind (see Genesis 6:13, 9:1, 15:13, 17:1). He required different functions of different families. For example, Noah and his family were the only family whom God requested to build an ark (see Genesis 6:13-14). During this time, each patriarch performed priestly functions for his household (see Genesis 8:20-9:1). The patriarchal dispensation ended when God gave the law to Moses on Mt. Sinai (see Exodus 19:20-25).

God's second period was the "Mosaic Dispensation." It began when God gave the law to Moses at Mt. Sinai (see Exodus 20:1-17), and it lasted approximately 1,500 years. During this dispensation, God made a covenant with Moses on behalf of and primarily for the Israelites (see verses 1-2). Through writing, God communicated the conditions of His covenant through the law of Moses, which included the ten commandments (see Exodus 20:1-17, Nehemiah 8:1-8). During this time, worship was basically confined to the tabernacle (see Exodus 25:8-9, 29:42-46, Hebrews 8:2-5, 9:2), the temple (see 1 Kings 6:11-13), and later the synagogue (see Luke 4:16). The *tabernacle* was a portable tent that was forty-five feet long by fifteen feet wide. While the Israelites wandered in the wilderness, this served as their place to offer sacrifices and worship. The *synagogue* was a place of worship in each Jewish community. It came into being while the Israelites were in captivity. The *temple* was a permanent structure erected in Jerusalem. It was the central place where all Jews went to worship, offer sacrifices, and study the law.

During this time, man, a mere human being, served as high priest for the people. Daily the priest offered sacrifices for his and the peoples' unintentional sins (see Leviticus 4:13-35, 5:14-19, Hebrews 5:1-4, 9:1-6, 10:11). Once per year, on the Day of Atonement (the tenth day of the seventh month), the high priest offered sacrifices for all other (intentional) of his and the peoples' sins (see Leviticus 16:15-34, Hebrews 9:7). This dispensation ended when God resurrected Jesus and sent the Holy Spirit on the day of Pentecost (see Acts 1:2-2:47).

God's third period is the "Christian Dispensation." It has lasted till the present. It began at the resurrection of Jesus Christ and the coming of the Holy Spirit on the day of Pentecost (see Acts 1:2-2:47). During this time, God made a covenant with His Son, Jesus Christ, on behalf of and toward all human beings (see Acts 3:22, Hebrews 8:6-12). God communicated the conditions of this covenant through Jesus Christ and the truths that are contained in the New Testament (see John 1:16-17). During this dispensation, true worship is never confined to a physical place, but a spiritual location, in Christ (see John 4:24). Jesus Christ, who was both human and divine, serves as our high priest for the people (see Hebrews 3:1-6, 7:12). The priest provided sacrifices for sin and access to God for the people. This dispensation continues into the present.

The law had not always been in effect. God had governed humankind without the law of Moses. He governed Moses for more than eighty years without the Law, for Moses was more than eighty years old when God revealed the Law to him at Mt. Sinai (see Exodus 7:7, Acts 7:23-30).

God added the law because of the waywardness of humankind. By attaching penalties to sin, the law increased awareness of sin. Even the ten commandments ordered punishment for its violators (see Exodus 35:1-3, Numbers 15:32-36). How many people would drive the speed limit if there were no penalty (fine) for speeding? Penalties increase our awareness of violations of the law.

The law was designed to last until the seed came (see Galatians 3:19). Jesus Christ was that seed (see verse 16). The law was designed to last until Jesus came into the world. It brought us to Christ, and then Christ released us from the law (see verses 24-25). We are children of God by faith in Jesus Christ, not by the law of Moses (see verses 26-27).

Thought Provokers

1. What would you say to someone who argues that the Bible was written by men?

2. What are the three dispensations, and where do you see yourself?

3. As a result of reading this chapter, how has your understanding changed regarding the law?

⇾ CHAPTER 8 ⇽

THE BIBLE OF GOD: THE INSPIRATION OF SCRIPTURE

MY GOD GAVE THE BIBLE WRITERS THEIR MESSAGE. THAT is what they claimed. They also said that God governed the transmission of it to humankind (see 2 Peter 1:19-21). Emphatically, they claimed that their message was accurate (see Psalm 19:7-8, 2 Timothy 3:14-17). Passing the test of intense scrutiny, indeed the Bible has proven itself to be archaeologically, historically, and scientifically true.

How can fallible men write an infallible Bible? Fallible men wrote the infallible earlier scripture because an infallible God superintended the process (see Jeremiah 36:2, 4, 17-18, 27, 32). No doubt, Jeremiah did and said some stupid things, but God never allowed him to clutter up the Bible with his personal errors. Fallible men wrote the infallible later scripture because an infallible God superintended the process (see Ephesians 3:1-7).

The Bible itself claims to be a product of the mind of God (see 2 Peter 1:21). Wisdom contained in scripture proves that the Bible is of supernatural origin. For example, the Bible was not written to be a treaty on medicine. However, the incidental medical wisdom in scripture proves that the Bible is of supernatural origin.

Early medicine did not enjoy the accepted and professional status that it now enjoys. It closely aligned itself and identified with pagan religions and superstitions because many attributed illness to the angry gods and evil spirits. Therefore, people used mystic rituals to appease the gods and ward off demons thought to cause disease and illnesses. The germ theory, the principle that explained the cause of infectious disease, evolved in the nineteenth century. In 1876, a German bacteriologist, Robert Koch, proved that a bacterium caused the disease anthrax. The theory's acceptance led to improved health practices including quarantine. Quarantine helps reduce death from plagues caused by germs and harmful bacteria. Quarantining individuals stops the spread of germs from the sick to the healthy. God's people had long ago practiced quarantine (see Leviticus 13:1-6, 8, 34, 52-59). Before modern medical discoveries, how could mankind have known to quarantine (see verse 46)? How did they know to quarantine? An all-wise God informed them.

There are other examples. In 1935, Professor Henrik Dam proposed the name "vitamin K" for the factor in foods that helped prevent hemorrhaging in baby chicks. We now know that vitamin K is responsible for the production of prothrombin by the liver.

If someone is deficient in vitamin K, they will also be deficient in prothrombin, and hemorrhaging may occur. It is very interesting to learn that vitamin K begins to be produced in a newborn male only during the fifth through seventh days of life (the vitamin is usually produced by bacteria in the intestinal tract). And it is only on the eighth day of life that the level of the blood-clotting element prothrombin is at 100 percent. God instructed Abraham to circumcise each male child on the eighth day (see Genesis 17:12). Why the eighth day? The best day for circumcision is, of course, the eighth day when the level of the blood-clotting element prothrombin is at 100 percent. How did Abraham know this with his limited scientific knowledge? It was not a lucky guess. An all-wise God informed him.

There are still other examples. We can live a few weeks without food, and a few days without water, but only a few moments without oxygen. Because of hemoglobin, red blood cells carry oxygen to each cell and make life possible. When oxygen-rich blood fails to reach cells, they die. Long before modern medical discovery, Moses knew that life was in the blood (see Leviticus 17:10-14). How could Moses have known that life was in the blood? An all-wise God informed him. He could not have known except for the divine wisdom of God given to him.

The English astronomer Edmund Halley (1656-1742) announced that water evaporates from the land and ocean, then condenses and falls as precipitation. The water that falls over land either returns to the air by evaporation or plant transpiration, or it flows back to the sea. This ceaseless movement is called the water cycle. Thousands of years before Halley, God's people knew of this hydrologic cycle (see Ecclesiastes 11:3, Amos 9:6). How did they know that the clouds contained the water from the sea? An all-wise God informed them. Wisdom contained in scripture proves that the Bible is of supernatural origin.

British scientist James Clerk Maxwell discovered that electricity and light waves were two forms of the same thing. He came to understand that all electromagnetic radiation from radio waves to x-rays travels at the speed of light. This is why we are able to have instantaneous wireless communication with someone on the other side of the earth. The fact that light could be sent and then manifest itself in speech wasn't discovered by science until 1864, but some 3,000 years earlier, God asked Job a strange question: "Can you send forth lightnings, that they may go and say to you, 'Here we are'?" (Job 38:35). Praise God that we now know that light can be sent, and then manifest itself in speech.

THE UNDERSTANDING OF SCRIPTURE

The sixty-six books of the Bible contain many and varied promises, requirements, and covenants—yet the message that the Bible presents for all mankind is unified. Within it, God has carried His people through several major transitions. Bridging the gap between transitions often requires tedious work, and the question becomes how much of the previous covenant or administration should find its way into the new administration.

The Bible of God: The Inspiration of Scripture

For too long, too many have believed that God authorizes believers to practice in the new (present) covenant none of what He authorized to practice in the old (former) covenant unless He had the practice re-taught (that is, specifically taught again) and brought into the new (present) covenant. I would propose, however, that God authorizes believers to practice in the new (present) covenant all of what He authorized to practice in the old (former) covenant unless He had the practice specifically removed by the teachings of the new (present) covenant.

What God commanded for the former covenant, He approves for the present covenant unless He disapproves it within the new covenant. What God approved for the former covenant, He appreciates for the present covenant unless He disregards it within the new covenant. What God appreciated for the former covenant, He allows for within the present covenant unless He disallows for it within the new covenant. Yes, God authorizes to practice according to the later scripture (New Covenant) all of what He authorized to practice according to the earlier scripture (Old Testament) unless He had the practice specifically removed by the teachings of the later scripture.

Within the former covenant, God provided specific dietary restrictions (see Leviticus 11:1-23, Acts 10:14). However, within the present covenant, God released those restrictions (see Acts 10:13-15). Therefore, the apostle Paul indicated that no judgment should come upon anyone because of their dietary habits (see Romans 14:3, Colossians 2:16-23).

Within the former covenant and within the context of addressing social concerns, God inserted a principle that just seems to be out of place. At the least, it is inconsistent with the flow of previous and subsequent thought within the passage (see Deuteronomy 25:4). We later learn that God included it not just for what it said then, but so that it would be applied among believers within the church (see 1 Corinthians 9:8-14, 1 Timothy 5:18). Obviously, this principle from the former covenant continued into the present covenant even before it had been stated within written scripture.

When the apostle Paul addressed the issue of rebellious women (church leaders' wives) within the church, he reminded them how principles from the former covenant also spoke to the situation (see 1 Corinthians 14:34). Within the present covenant, believers are redeemed from the curse of the law (see Galatians 3:10-14). Everything within the law was not a curse. Therefore, we are not released from the principles of the teachings of the law but rather the curse of the Law (death). For example, God admonishes fathers to bring up their children in the discipline and instructions of the Lord (see Ephesians 6:4). Where within our present covenant do we find specifics? Will we ever find better specifics than those from the former covenant (such as Deuteronomy 6:1-25)?

Consider our own experiences for a moment. Let us say that we worked under the jurisdiction of one administration or supervisor who was then replaced by another. Do we immediately cease all policies and procedures that the former administration or supervisor had authorized? Certainly not. Likely, we would continue to follow the exact same previously authorized policies and procedures until we were informed to cease or amend them. Now, we may renege on some of the policies and procedures that we detested, but in general we would follow the same ones as we followed under the old administration.

Apply that same ideology to changing from the former covenant to our present covenant. Most likely the believers continued participating according to the same principles they had previously followed. We now know why the apostle Peter in his vision refused so staunchly even to consider eating animals that were unclean under the former covenant (see Acts 10:9-16). Without direct intervention from God, he never would have changed that former covenant principle (see Acts 11:5-9). Also, we now know why the apostles so strongly refused to give up the requirement of circumcision; they carried former covenant principles into the present covenant until they were specifically removed (see Acts 15:1-29).

Within the present covenant, believers continued to make vows (see Acts 18:18) and observe Pentecost in Jerusalem (see Acts 20:16, 1 Corinthians 16:8). These practices came from the former covenant. They continued to practice the policies and procedures of the former covenant until they were specifically removed.

Why, then, are the policies and procedures of the former covenant, which have not been specifically removed by the teachings of the present covenant, not valid for us? We must work to obtain a proper understanding of scripture. There exists a specific meaning of the text. The specific meaning of the text depends on the specific conscious will of the author. Therefore, the specific meaning of the text is that pattern of meaning that the author consciously willed to convey. The author determined the meaning of the text. In the past, when the text was written, he willed that meaning of the text. The meaning of the text is historical. The meaning of the text can never change. The meaning of the text is forever locked in history. Even the author cannot recant the meaning of the text (see Galatians 1:8-9). The goal of biblical understanding is to understand the specific meaning.

There are implications within the text. The implications of the text are the non-conscious will of the author. Very likely the author knew not all the implications of the text. The prophets themselves desired to understand better. They recognized that often they did not understood the very prophecies they provided (see 1 Peter 1:10-12). Therefore, the implications are the meanings in a text of which the author may be unaware, but nevertheless fall legitimately within the willed pattern of meaning. The specific meaning of the text determines the implications of the text. In the present, while the text is being examined, the implications become exposed. The meaning is singular and historical, while the implications are numerous and contemporary. The implications of the text can change. The implications are fluid.

In each text there is a specific meaning and various implications. The specific meaning of the text is, "Do not drink wine to the excess" (see Ephesians 5:18). The implication is, "Avoid intoxicating beverages." Did the apostle Paul know that Jack Daniels whiskey would be distilled? I doubt that he did. Would he have willed to prohibit intoxication by whiskey? Very likely he would have.

The goal of biblical understanding is to understand the specific meaning and the various implications. They are not determined by the interpreter. They are determined by the author. There exists the significance of the text. The significance is how the reader responds to the meaning and implications of the text. Those who believe may attribute positive significance, while those who disbelieve may attribute negative significance to the meaning of the text. Significance is a critique of the author's pattern of meaning. It is the effect that the text's meaning has on the reader. Since Christians believe that the Word is from God, it should always have a positive significance for believers. Meaning belongs to the author. Significance belongs to the reader. There is one meaning, several implications, and multifaceted significance.

In view of this, let us analyze Matthew 28:19-20: "Go therefore and make disciples of all the nations, baptizing them in the name of the Father and the Son and the Holy Spirit, teaching them to observe all that I commanded you; and lo, I am with you always, even to the end of the age." The text means that the eleven disciples were to go and make disciples of all nations. The text implies that all believers must inform others of the good news of the gospel of Christ. Its significance to me personally is that I must conduct home Bible studies, enroll others in a Bible correspondence course, invite people to hear the gospel preached, etc.

Significance consists of all the positive responses to the legitimate implications of the text. Significance is the manner in which we obey the implications of the text. Significance for one person may differ from the significance for another person. The text consists of words, which are shareable symbols. The reader must become familiar with the meaning of the shareable symbols in order to understand the text. Four responsible actions will help us to do this:

1. Examine the precept of the passage. What exactly does the scripture say? What exactly does the scripture state? The disciples misunderstood what Jesus stated (see John 21:18-23). Jesus never said that the disciples would not die. What exactly does the scripture imply? This text implies that only believers should be baptized (see Acts 8:31-37). Also, it implies that those who do not believe and those who are incapable of believing are not candidates for baptism.

2. Examine the purpose of the passage. Exactly what was the reason for the writing? Single or multiple purposes may exist. Sometimes the purpose is stated. The apostle Paul wrote so that the evangelist Timothy would know how to govern within the church (see 1 Timothy 3:14-15). Other passages state their purpose (see 1 John 1:4, 2:1, 12-14, 21, 5:13). Sometimes the purpose is implied. Certain behaviors please God and keep us from falling (see 2 Peter 1:11, 17).

3. Examine the principle of the passage. Exactly what fundamental rule or principle is always true? For example, we should always celebrate when the lost is found (see Luke 15:1-32). God celebrates; therefore, we should always celebrate when the lost is found. We should always pursue peace (see Romans 14:1-19). Pursing peace may require us to accept the immature without judgment.

4. Examine the precedent of the passage. Exactly what acceptable and authorized trends exist? God designated male leadership within the church. He addressed women problems through men (see Acts 6:1-3, Philippians 1:1, 4:2-3, 1 Timothy 2:12-13). Before the time of Jesus, instruments of music were found in abundance in the praise

ceremonies. After the time of Jesus, they seemed no longer to exist (see Matthew 26:30, Acts 16:25, Hebrews 2:12, 13:15). There are some who suggest that the Greek word for "sing psalms" (Strong's #G5567 and #G5568) suggests the idea of instrumental music (see Ephesians 5:19, Colossians 3:16, 1 Corinthians 14:15, James 5:13). The weight of scholarly authority is against it. Early reformers such as Martin Luther, John Wycliffe, William Tyndale, Thomas Crammer, and Dean Alford argue against instrumental music. When we understand the stated purpose for singing, we should have no problem just singing.

Thought Provokers

1. If someone tells you that the Bible cannot be infallible because it was written by fallible men, how would you reply?

2. As a result of reading this chapter, how has your understanding changed regarding the transition from "former covenant" to "present covenant"?

3. List the four responsible actions that will help you to understand the meaning of a text.

CHAPTER 9

THE SALVATION OF GOD

MY GOD, THROUGH JESUS CHRIST, OFFERS SALVATION TO all of us. Salvation is a deliverance from an old relationship to a new relationship. This deliverance takes place according to an authorized process.

THE UNIVERSALITY OF SIN

Adam introduced sin into the world (see Romans 5:12). Declaring their independence from God, Adam and Eve attempted to live independently of God's instructions (see Genesis chapters 2-3). Attempting to live independently of God introduced sin to the world (see 1 John 3:4). Ever since then, sin has woven itself into the very fabric of human existence (see Romans 3:23). Sin permeates every aspect of humanity. Sin corrupts our character.

There is none righteous, not even one; there is none who understands, there is none who seeks for God; all have turned aside, together they have become useless; there is none who does good, there is not even one. Their throat is an open grave, with their tongues they keep deceiving, the poison of asps is under their lips" (Romans 3:10-13; see also Psalm 14:1-3).

In the verses from Romans, the Holy Spirit used the words *no one*, *none*, and *not even one* six times in three short verses. Sin causes us to become characteristically ignorant. "There is none who understands" (verse 11). Educated people just cannot seem to understand the problems with abortion, homosexuality, and fornication. Sin causes us to become characteristically useless (see verse 12). This word described milk that had become contaminated and spoiled, needing to be thrown away.

Sin corrupts our conversation. "The throat is an open grave" (Romans 3:13a; also see Matthew 12:34-36, 15:11, 18). Graves contain rotting flesh that produces rotten odor. Sin causes us to become conversationally deceptive (see Romans 3:13b, Psalm 5:9). Some lie in word, action, and satisfaction. Sin causes us to become conversationally destructive (see Romans 3:13c-14, Mark 11:12-14, 20-21, Luke 9:54, Psalm 140:1-3). Sin flows from the heart, through the throat, over the tongue, by the lips, and out of the mouth, resulting in total contamination.

Sin corrupts our conduct (see Roman 3:15). We do not always express the ultimate of our inwardness (see Matthew 5:21-28). Sin causes us to become actively cruel (see Roman 3:16). Sin causes us to become passively cruel (see Roman 3:17).

Christians should recognize the permeating principle of sin (see 1 John 1:8). Ever since Adam and Eve brought sin into the world (see Romans 5:12), it has weaved itself into the very fabric of human existence. Everyone has experienced sin (see Romans 3:23). We must recognize that there is a past penalty for sins (see Romans 6:23). The past penalty for sin is eternal death (see Genesis 2:16-17, Romans 5:12, 6:16, 21, 23). Eternal death is an eternal separation from God Himself (see 2 Thessalonians 1:6-10). We must recognize that there is a present power of sin (see Romans 6:16-20). The present power of sin is its dominating enslavement (see Genesis 4:7, Romans 6:14, 18, 22). Dominating enslavement is an allowance from God Himself (see Romans 6:16-19).

Christians should resist the possible preference to sin (see 1 John 2:1). We do not have to sin (see 1 Corinthians 10:13, Romans 6:13-14), but we probably will sin. We must continually make decisions, and often we make wrong decisions. We often make decisions that are anti-scriptural. We simply possess a strong inclination to sin. Being ignorant, we often fail to resist sin (see Acts 3:14-17, Romans 10:3, 14:1-13, 1 Timothy 1:13). Being rebellious, we often fail to resist sin (see Romans 1:18-25, Jude 11).

As Christians, we should receive the powerful propitiation for our sin (see 1 John 2:2). Jesus is the propitiation (satisfaction) for our sin. Our good deeds are not the satisfaction. Jesus has already satisfied God's demand for our sin. God cannot, therefore, not tolerate sin. Someone had to pay the penalty. Jesus died on the cross for us (see Ephesians 2:16, Colossians 1:20). Jesus is the propitiation for sins; therefore, we must not deny sin (see 1 John 1:10). The basic human problem is man disagreeing with God. We disagree that sin is present and also on how to purge it. We call it an accident, but God calls it an abomination. We call it a fascination, but God calls it a fatality. We call it liberty, but God calls it lawlessness.

Jesus is the propitiation for sins; therefore we must confess it (see 1 John 1:8-9). To confess is to speak the same thing as another. When God holds the charge of sin against us, we must say about our sins what God says about our sins. God says that we are guilty; we must, therefore, say we are guilty (see Psalm 32). Divine forgiveness becomes divine forgetfulness (see Hebrews 10:17). When man holds the charge of sin against us, we must say about our sins what others say about our sins. When man says that we are guilty, we must agree (see Luke chapter 15).

FORGIVENESS

The preaching of the death, burial, and resurrection of Jesus Christ resulted in people becoming forgiven of sins (see Acts 2:36-38). The preaching of the death, burial, and resurrection of Jesus Christ resulted in people becoming saved (see Acts 2:47). The preaching of the death, burial, and resurrection of Jesus Christ resulted in people becoming members of the church (see Acts 2:47).

Becoming forgiven of sins is equivalent to becoming saved, which is equivalent to becoming a member of the church. Those who are forgiven have become saved. Those who are saved are members of the church. One cannot become a member of the church without becoming saved. One cannot become saved without becoming a member of the church. So, to be saved is to be in the church, and to be in the church is the same as being saved.

The church, the body of Christ, came to exist only after the resurrection of Jesus. Christianity rises and/or falls on the resurrection of Jesus. The resurrection is more than a contemporary Easter idea; it is the very essence of Christianity. Christians pledge themselves not to a festive holiday program, but to a person, the resurrected Lord Jesus Christ. The message of the death, burial, and resurrection of Jesus brought the church into existence. An appropriate response of faith toward the death, burial, and resurrection of Jesus brings a person into a forgiven state, saved, and into the church.

Believing that Jesus is the Christ, the Son of God, is an adequate response of faith. The death, burial, and resurrection of Jesus proves that He is the Christ, the Son of God (see Romans 1:1-4, Acts 17:30-31). Therefore, only those who believe can become forgiven of sins, saved, and members of the church (see John 8:24, Acts 4:1-4, 8:35-37). Repenting of sin is an adequate response of faith. Repentance is the change of heart within a person (see Matthew 21:28-32). In repentance, we change our allegiance (see Acts 2:38, 17:30, 26:19-20). We remove our allegiance to our selfish self, and we pledge our allegiance to the Savior.

Becoming baptized is an adequate response of faith. Baptism is our response to the call of God (see 1 Peter 3:21). Near the beginning of his ministry, the apostle Peter preached about baptism. Near the end of his ministry, the apostle Peter wrote about baptism. Even now, baptism saves. What is baptism?

First, we consider the dry side of baptism. It is a response of the mind, for it is an internal appeal toward God. The dry side is a response of the conscience. The conscience is a product of accepted teachings (see John 8:1-9, Leviticus 20:10). The dry side is a response of a *good* conscience. Within this context, a good conscience is a heart that trusts in the resurrection of Jesus Christ (see 1 Peter 3:21). The resurrection proves that Jesus is the Son of God (see Romans 1:4, Acts 17:31). Only those who believe in the resurrection of Jesus have a good conscience for baptism (see John 8:24, Acts 8:35-37). If our conscience is insufficiently taught, our conscience will be insufficiently developed. And if our conscience is incorrectly taught, then it will be incorrectly developed.

Baptism takes place while the penitent believer is in water (see Acts 8:36-39). Baptism consists of taking the penitent believer to the water, and never bringing the water to the penitent believer. We should never attempt to reduce baptism to sprinkling and pouring of water. Some object to the necessity of being covered in water, but Jesus was sealed in His tomb (see Matthew 27:62-64, Romans 6:4). Some object to the necessity of water, yet water is specifically mentioned (see Acts 8:36-39, 10:47, 1 Peter 3:20-21). God refused to heal Naaman until he went into the water (see 2 Kings 5:14).

When those who heard the gospel believed, repented, and became baptized, they were forgiven, saved, and became members of the church. Even now, a faith response to the death, burial, and resurrection of Jesus Christ allows one to become forgiven of sins, saved, and a Christian.

ETERNAL SECURITY

The apostle John wrote to those who believed in the name (authority, character, reputation) of Jesus Christ. His writing reassured them of the surety of their salvation (see 1 John 5:13). Even now, the saved are eternally secure. Remember that salvation is a military concept that means a deliverance from an old relationship of danger to a new relationship of safety.

We are saved from the *past penalty* of sin. The past penalty of sin is death. Through Jesus Christ, God reversed the eternal consequences of sin, thereby saving us from death (see Romans 6:23).

We are saved from the *present power* of sin. The present power of sin is domination. Through Jesus Christ, God equips us to reduce the dominance of sin in our lives (see 1 Peter 5:6-9, James 4:7, Ephesians 3:20-21, 4:27, 6:11).

We are saved from the *future presence* of sin. The future presence of sin is absence from the presence of God (see Genesis 4:16). Absence from the presence of God is a decision of God Himself (see 2 Thessalonians 1:6-10). Through Jesus Christ, God will nullify His previous decision and bring us eternally into His eternal presence (see Romans 6:23).

We are eternally secure because God has saved us (see 1 Peter 1:3). Because of His mercy, God saved us (see 1 Peter 1:3, Titus 3:4-5). Mercy is a special and immediate regard to eliminate the misery of another. Because of His grace, God saved us (see 2 Timothy 1:8-10). Grace is our license to receive forgiveness of sins.

We are eternally secure because God keeps us saved (see 1 Peter 1:5, 2 Peter 2:4-10, Philippians 1:6). By His discipline, God keeps us saved (see 1 Peter 1:5-9, Hebrews 12:3-11). By His directions, God keeps us saved (see 2 Peter 1:1-11).

We are saved because God saved us through Jesus Christ (see Matthew 1:19-23, Luke 19:10, Romans 5:1-2). Through Jesus Christ, God paid the past penalty for sin (see 2 Corinthians 5:19, 21, Romans 4:8). The past penalty of sin is death (see 2 Thessalonians 1:6-10). Through Jesus Christ, God provided peace from sin (see 2 Corinthians 5:17-21). Peace is freedom from the distresses of sin.

We are saved because God keeps us saved through Jesus Christ (see John 10:27-30, Romans 8:35-39, Isaiah 43:13). Through Jesus Christ, God provides power over sin (see Romans 6:8-14, 8:1-3). Through Jesus Christ, God provides a place from sin (see Romans 6:3-7).

God saved us by the Holy Spirit. By the Holy Spirit, God convinced us to become saved (see John 16:8-11). He convinced us that we are guilty of sin (see John 16:8). We are guilty of sin because of our unbelief (see John 16:9). The word of God is the scalpel that the Holy Spirit uses to perform open heart surgery within the sinner (see Ephesians 6:17). Through His word, God convinces sinners to believe and become saved (see Acts 2:37, 8:12, 11:14).

God keeps us saved by the Holy Spirit. By the Holy Spirit, God conditions our hearts to remain saved (see John 16:8-11). He conditions us to live guiltless of sin (see John 16:8). We are guiltless because of the resurrection of Jesus (see John 16:10). The word of

God is the scalpel that the Holy Spirit uses to perform open heart surgery within the saint (see Hebrews 4:12). Through His word, God conditions the saint to continue to believe and remain saved (see Romans 6:1-8, 8:1-2, 16-17, 33-34, Ephesians 5:18, 6:10-16).

We can be sure of our salvation. God keeps us saved on the basis of His grace, not because of our good works (see Romans 4:1-13, Genesis 15:6, Titus 3:4-7, Ephesians 2:4-10). God saved us to do good works, not because of our good works (see 2 Timothy 1:8-12). Does this mean we should not work? No, but rather we must work. Work is the indicator of a healthy faith (see James 2:14-26). Therefore, we must work out our salvation (see Philippians 2:12). What does it mean to work out our salvation? To work out means to manifest outwardly what God has placed inwardly (see Philippians 1:6, Romans 5:3, 15:18, 2 Corinthians 7:10-11, James 1:3, 20). Their salvation resulted not from a work of man for God, but rather their salvation resulted from a work of God for man—accomplished through the blood of Jesus Christ.

We are eternally secure because God saved us in spite of the fact that we had sinned in the past. Yes, God knows our past, and He saved us in spite of the fact that we have sinned (see Romans 3:23, 5:6-12, 6:17-18, 1 Corinthians 6:11, Acts 2:36-47, 22:8-16).

We are eternally secure because God keeps us saved in spite of the fact that we will sin in the future. Yes, God knows our future, and He keeps us saved in spite of the fact that we will sin again. God prepares us to avoid sin (see 1 John 2:1a). God provides for our forgiveness when we do sin (see 1 John 2:1b-2, 1:6-7, 9). For whom is forgiveness available? Forgiveness is available for those who walk in the light and confess (see 1 John 1:7, 9). What does it mean to walk in the light? Contextually to walk in the light means to love your brother (see 1 John 2:9-11, John 13:34-35, Matthew 5:44-48). What does it mean to confess? Confess means to agree in the heart and speak the same thing as another (see 1 John 1:10).

Will God forgive those who live less than sinless perfect lives? Yes, forgiveness is available for those who live less than sinless, perfect lives. Often, Christians become upset when they learn that God will forgive those who live less than sinless, perfect lives. Deep in their hearts, they know that they will be saved only if God saves them. God will save them in spite of the fact that they are never going to live sinless, perfect lives. God's saving power reaches us while we are less than perfect.

Speak confidently of the security of our salvation. Believers have been justified by faith. To be justified is to be declared righteous. Faith is what one does about what one believes that God has said (see 2 Corinthians 4:13). Believers who are justified by faith possess peace. Peace is the absence of the distresses that are caused by sin. This peace is in the present tense indicating that it is here and now. What does this peace provide? It provides the benefit of knowing that salvation is forever. Peace provides access to God (see Romans 5:1-2). We have obtained an introduction by faith into this grace of peace (see Ephesians 2:18, 3:12). Grace is a license to receive all the spiritual blessings of God. Our access is permanent. In that grace we stand (see Romans 5:2). Our access is pleasurable. In that grace we exult and rejoice (see Romans 5:2). Peace provides assurance (see Romans 5:3-4). Our assurance displays the fact (see Romans 5:3a).

The Salvation of God

We exult in tribulation. Tribulation is a squeezing together. Our assurance develops fruit (see Romans 5:3b-4).

Believers who are justified by faith possess peace. Peace provides a permanent place in the presence of God. By the cross of Jesus, God demonstrated His love for us (see Romans 5:6-8). He injected His love into our heart (see Romans 5:5). Therefore, the apostle Paul lifted up love as an unbreakable link in the chain of salvation for the justified believer.

Our spiritual love relationship with God lasts throughout all eternity. Because of His love, God brings sinners to grace (see Romans 5:6-9a). Grace is a license to receive all that God provides. Therein, we are justified in His blood. Initially, our salvation is a provision of the love of God. God loved us when we were sinners (see John 3:16). Because of His love, God brings saints to glory (see Romans 5:9b-11). Therefore, we are identified in His body. Subsequently, our salvation is a product of the love of God. If He loved us when we were enemies (sinners), does He now love us any less as friends (saints)?

Because they have no conscious feelings of hatred and do not actively oppose Him, many do not see themselves as enemies to God. They believe that they are neutral, but that is not possible (see Luke 11:23). It is only after conversion that we become no longer children of wrath (see Ephesians 2:3, 1 Thessalonians 1:10, 5:9). God guarantees our salvation. He guarantees our salvation on the basis of the past work of Christ on the cross. He guarantees our salvation on the basis of the present work of Christ at the right hand of the Father.

Thought Provokers

1. How has your understanding of sin changed as a result of studying this chapter?

2. How has your understanding of forgiveness and salvation changed as a result of studying this chapter?

3. What does this statement mean to you: "Grace is a license to receive all that God provides."

※ CHAPTER 10 ※

THE CHURCH OF GOD: THE UNIVERSAL CHURCH

MY GOD HAS ALWAYS GATHERED HIS PEOPLE. HE HAS gathered His people socially, intellectually, and geographically. He gathered Adam and Eve into the Garden of Eden (see Genesis 2:15-25), Noah and his family into the ark (see Genesis 7:1-7), Abraham and his family into the land of Canaan (see Genesis 12:5), Jacob and all his descendants into the land of Egypt (see Genesis 46:1-6), Moses and all of Israel into the clouds and the Red Sea to be baptized unto Him (see Exodus 14:21-22, 1 Corinthians 10:1-4), and David and all of Israel at the crossing of the Jordan River (see 2 Samuel 10:17).

THE UNIVERSAL CHURCH

Now, God gathers all His people into the church of Christ (see Ephesians 1:20-23, 2:4-7, 3:20-21, Acts 2:47). Within the church, God provides for human participation within the divine scheme of redemption (see 2 Corinthians 5:17-21). Therefore, the church is God's gracious gathering. The church is further God's gracious universal gathering. He gathers His people into the universal church. The universal church is God's gracious gathering for reconciliation and relationship (see Ephesians 1:22-23, 2:12-16, 19).

Within scripture, a distinct organism called the church came to exist. Before the death, burial, and resurrection of Jesus Christ, scripture declared that the church *would* come into existence (see Matthew 16:18). After the death, burial, and resurrection of Jesus Christ, scripture declared that the church had *already* come into existence (see Acts 8:1-3). The preaching of the death, burial, and resurrection of Jesus Christ resulted in people becoming forgiven of sins (see Acts 2:36-38), saved (see Acts 2:47), and members of the church. Therefore, becoming forgiven of sin is equivalent to becoming saved, which is equivalent to becoming a member of the church. The message of the death, burial, and resurrection of Jesus Christ brought the church into existence. A response of faith to the death, burial, and resurrection of Jesus Christ causes one to become forgiven of sins, saved, and a member of the church. What is an adequate response of faith? Adequate responses of faith include:

Believing that Jesus is the Christ, the Son of God, is an adequate response of faith. The death, burial, and resurrection prove that Jesus is the Christ, the Son of God (see Acts 15:7). Since Jesus is the

Son of God, what He says is true. Therefore, only those who believe that Jesus is the Christ, the Son of God, can become forgiven of sins, saved, and members of the church (see Acts 8:35-39).

Repenting of sin is an adequate response of faith (see Acts 17:30). Repentance is a change of mind that takes place in our heart. We must change our minds about sin and about Jesus as the Son of God. In repentance, we accepted what we had neglected and/or rejected relative to God's standard.

Becoming baptized is an adequate response of faith, for it is our response to the call of God (see 1 Peter 3:21). Baptism takes place while a penitent believer is in the water (see Acts 8:36-39). When we believe, repent, and are baptized, we become forgiven, saved, and members of the church.

God intends for all of His people to be one (see John 17:21). Scripture calls the body the church (see Ephesians 1:22-23). Seeing that there is just one body, there must also just be one church (see Ephesians 4:4). The church is the one family of God. All God's children are within His family (see 1 Corinthians 12:12-14, 20, 27). There are no Christians outside the church.

God created one human family (see Genesis 3:20, Acts 17:26, 1 Corinthians 15:39). There are many members of the human family. Often we refer to a sub-unit (specific family) as a family. What are the criteria for becoming a member of the human family?

If Stevie Wonder adopts a seeing-eye dog, gives him a name, provides him a salary, opens a bank account for him, obtains a social security number for him, and trains him to do housework, is the dog a member of the human family? No! Why not? The dog is not a member of the human family because he has never been born into the human family. Life-long association with a sub-unit (the Wonder family) never qualifies the dog to be a member of the human family. Only through birth can one become a member of the human family. Affiliation with a sub-unit never qualifies one to become a member of the human family.

God created one church. Often we refer to a sub-unit (specific congregation) as a church. What is the criteria for becoming a member of the church? If Stevie brings his seeing-eye dog to the assembly, is his dog a member of the church? If the dog participates in the worship services, is the dog a member? No! Why not? The dog is not a member of the church because he has never been added to the church by the Lord (see Acts 2:47). Life-long association with a sub-unit (specific congregation) never qualifies the dog to be a member of the church. Only through being born again and being added by the Lord can one become a member of the church of Christ. Affiliation with a religious group never qualifies one to become a member of the church of Christ.

The church of Christ is the family of God (see Ephesians 3:15). Family denotes relationship. If, then, the church is a family, then those within the church share a relationship with God. God is Father and we are His children. The children of God share a relationship with each other. We are brothers and sisters in Christ. Yes, those within the church are spiritual relatives, all related by the blood of Jesus. Those in the church are redeemed by the blood of Christ and are born again into a state of innocence and holiness (see 1 Peter 1:13-23). Yet, the church consists not of perfect people, but purified people. One is born again and purified by obeying the truth (see 1 Peter 1:22). This could only happen to those who had been taught the truth (see Romans 6:17, John 6:44-45).

The church consists of people who have responded favorably to the gospel of Christ. They have been born again into the family of God. We can be born again, a Christian, and a relative in the family of God without ever being part of any denomination (see Romans 6:17-18, 1 Corinthian 12:12). In spite of the diversity of the members within the church, the church as the body of Christ is one (see 1 Corinthians 12:12-13). All who are disciples therein are members of one body, the church.

THE NATURE OF THE UNIVERSAL CHURCH

God established His covenant with Moses for the Israelites (see Exodus 19:1-8). Then God provided guidelines to govern their responses toward Him and other individuals (see Exodus 20:1-22, chapters 12-17). Surely, the Israelites were the covenanted people of God.

God promised to make a new covenant with a new covenant people (see Jeremiah 31:31, Hebrews 8:8-12, Deuteronomy 18:14-15, Acts 3:12-26). During the Mosaic dispensation, God had a house for His people, but during the Christian dispensation, God has a people for His house. The church of Christ contains God's new covenanted people.

The prophets of old predicted that God would provide a *new* institution of His people (see Isaiah 2:2-3, Micah 4:1-2, Zechariah 1:16). That new institution will be *international* (see Revelation 5:9), *interracial* (see Galatians 3:27-29), and *indestructible* (see Hebrews 12:28). The church is essentially one body, intentionally one body, and constitutionally one body.

The resurrection of Jesus secures forgiveness of sin, salvation, and a born-again status for us. Whom has God forgiven? God has forgiven those who have been baptized (see Mark 16:16, Acts 2:38, 1 Peter 3:21). What? Is that all? No! God has forgiven those who have been baptized because they believe that Jesus is the Christ, the Son of God. (see Acts 2:38, 8:37, 1 Peter 3:21). God has forgiven those who have been baptized because they believe that Jesus is the Christ, the Son of God, because they have heard the evidence (see John 20:31, Acts 17:31, Romans 1:4). In each account of conversion, Jesus is preached as the resurrected savior (see Acts 2:22-37).

When we experience the one baptism, we become a member of the one body of Christ, the one church of Christ (see Ephesians 1:22-23, 4:5). Once we are baptized into the one body of Christ, the one church of Christ, we never need to be baptized again. The misguided religious world advocates that baptism is in order to become a member within a sub-unit (specific congregation). Therefore, some are baptized thinking that they are baptized just to become a member within a particular fellowship. This idea is foreign to scripture. Being baptized into the one body of Christ, the one church of Christ, and becoming a member of a specific congregation are separate and distinct issues. Of what specific congregation was the eunuch a member (see Acts 8:26-39)?

The devil seeks to deny the essentiality of the church. Therefore, he seeks to make us believe that the church is non-essential. The devil seeks to distort the identity of the church. Therefore, he seeks to make us think and attempt to pattern the church after corporate America. The devil seeks to detract from our investment in the church. He seeks to give us the wrong motive when we utilize the right manner. He seeks to give us the right motive by the wrong manner.

How much must one know before becoming baptized? I favor teaching an abundance of truth, yet we must ask how much does the scripture indicate that believers knew before they became baptized? How can we know how much a person knows? We only know how much a person knows by how much they indicate that they know.

On Pentecost, Peter preached a powerful sermon designed to convict the audience of their guilt of the sin of crucifying Jesus (see Acts 2:22-38). They crucified Him because they did not believe that He was who He claimed to be. Their question (see Acts 2:37) indicated they had now come to believe that Jesus was the Son of God.

Beginning with the prophet Isaiah, the evangelist Phillip explained to the eunuch who Jesus was. The eunuch's affirmative answer to Phillip's question confirmed his belief that Jesus was the Son of God (see Acts 8:36-37). Upon receiving the confirmation of the eunuch's belief that Jesus was the Christ, Phillip baptized him. Phillip neither asked for nor received confirmation that the eunuch understood how to worship. Phillip neither asked for nor received confirmation that the eunuch would observe the Lord's Supper.

How much did believers indicate they knew before being baptized? They indicated only that they believed that Jesus was the Son of God (see Acts 8:37). Believers need to know how to worship, where to worship, the nature of the church, how to behave as a Christian, and more. Yet, believers were never called upon to demonstrate that level of knowledge prior to becoming baptized. Saying that one has become a Christian differs from saying that one has learned to behave as a Christian (see Matthew 28:18-20). Some have become Christians, yet are worshipping in error. We must call them out of all religious error.

Thought Provokers

1. Read John 17:21 and then meditate upon this statement: "God intends for all His people to be one."

2. Read Ephesians 3:15 and then meditate upon this statement: "The church of Christ is the family of God."

3. How has your understanding of the church of God changed as a result of your meditation of these verses and statements?

→ CHAPTER 11 ←

THE CHURCH OF GOD: THE LOCAL CHURCH

MY GOD HAD AN IDEA: THE LOCAL CHURCH. IT WAS HIS idea (see Acts 8:1-2, 9:26-28, Romans 16:1, 3-5, 10, 16). The local church is associated with a geographic region. It attracts its members from a specific geographic locality (see Acts 11:22, 13:1, 18:22, 20:17) and assembles its members at a specific geographic locality (see Acts 14:27, 20:7-8, 1 Corinthians 11:18-20, 14:23-26). The local church is a body of believers brought together by God at a specific geographic locality, entrusted to the God-ordained pastoral teaching of His knowledge and wisdom.

God ordained teachers (see Ephesians 4:11, 1 Corinthians 12:28-29). God ordained teachers to teach certain students. God ordained Philip to teach the eunuch (see Acts 8:26-40). God ordained Peter to teach Cornelius (see Acts 10:17-34). God ordained Ananias to teach

Saul (see Acts 22:6-16). God ordained Paul to teach the Gentiles (see Acts 22:17-21, 9:15). Within the church, there should be a God-ordained teacher who teaches the knowledge and wisdom of God (see 1 Timothy 2:1-7, 2 Timothy 1:8-11).

THE LOCAL CHURCH

The church exists as a universal body and as a local body of believers. Universally it is divided into individually structured or local churches or congregations. Every disciple of Christ should identify with a local congregation of the church of Christ. Each week, each local congregation should assemble and provide an opportunity for its members to glorify God and edify each other (see Hebrews 10:23-25).

The local church is a group of believers brought together by God at a specific geographic locality, entrusted to the God-ordained pastoral teaching of His knowledge and wisdom, so that believers can live out their covenant commitment to the corporate vision. Believers enter into a covenant commitment with the local church (see 1 Corinthians 12:18-27, Acts 9:26, 10:28, 2 Samuel 20:1-2). Believers live out their covenant commitment through the corporate vision of the local church (see 1 Thessalonians 5:12-13, Hebrews 13:17, 1 Peter 5:3, Acts 15:3). Every church does not have the same charge. Paul wrote, for example, about the extraordinary grace that the Macedonian church had for giving. "Now, brethren, we wish to make known to you the grace of God which has been given in the churches of Macedonia, that in a great ordeal of affliction their abundance of joy and their deep poverty overflowed in the wealth of their liberality" (2 Corinthians 8:1-2). The apostle Paul did not charge the Macedonians to give in this offering. They begged for the opportunity to participate. Another example is the vision that God gave to the apostle Peter, which the other apostles initially opposed (see Acts 10:17-11:1).

The local church consists of imperfect believers. God expects imperfect believers to fellowship and function with minimal friction at one geographic locality. We should consider God's desire for us, and let Him lead us to a local church. He knows whose teaching style fits our learning style and which vision best accommodates our spiritual gifts. God assigns vision based on the personnel He will lead to the local church. Never oppose a congregation just because it does not participate in a good work. It may be a good work but outside God's vision for them at that time. Likewise, the same should be true of individuals. Never oppose an individual just because he does not participate in a good work. It may be a good work but outside God's vision for him at that time.

Before entering a covenant commitment with another local church, we must be released from our previous covenant commitment from our present local church (see Acts 18:27, Romans 16:1, Colossians 4:10).

ACCOUNTABLE FUNCTION WITHIN THE LOCAL CHURCH

Every Christian should become a member of a local church, for by joining we become accountable (see Hebrews 13:17). Discover the local church's joining procedure and submit to it.

Every member in the local church should function within the local church. And each member of the church should have an assigned function within the local church. Through the analogy of the human body, God teaches some truths about the body of Christ—the local church (see 1 Corinthians 12:12). Which member of the body does not have an assigned function? Which member does not function toward the body's purposeful mission? Each member of the human body has an assigned function and does function toward the purposeful mission of that human body. Likewise, each member of the church should function faithfully according to the gift given by God (see 1 Peter 4:10-11). God has given at least one grace gift to each Christian (see 1 Peter 4:10a). We possess the gift but do not own the gift. God expects each Christian to serve faithfully as good stewards (see 1 Peter 4:10). A steward is one who is faithful (see 1 Corinthians 4:1-2), that is, fulfills assigned responsibilities (see Ephesians 6:21-22).

Members who do not function are dysfunctional. Dysfunctional members rob the body of its effectiveness. Dysfunctional members waste and disgrace God's grace gifts. Members of the church are not volunteers. Volunteers receive neither pleasurable compensations nor painful consequences for their service or lack of service. God provides pleasure for those who serve and pain for those who refuse to serve (see 2 Corinthians 5:9-10, Ephesians 6:8). Therefore, when we serve, we do ourselves, not God, a favor. God is not our "homeboy." For our homeboy, we do whatever we decide, whenever we decide to do it. To God, we have the power to say "no," but not the right to say "no." If we simply come, hear the word, and leave, we are out of order.

ACCOUNTABLE FELLOWSHIP WITHIN THE LOCAL CHURCH

Fellowship takes place when a compatible interest causes a compatible participation within a compatible activity and/or experience (see Acts 2:41-43, 1 Corinthians 1:9, 2 Corinthians 8:4, 13:14, Philippians 1:3-5, 3:10, 4:13-18, Philemon 6). Within the local church, each member should be moved by a compatible interest to participate compatibly within compatible activities and/or experiences.

Each member should connect to other members within the local church, "from whom the whole body, being fitted and held together by what every joint supplies, according to the proper working of each individual part, causes the growth of the body for the building up of itself in love" (Ephesians 4:16). Each member should establish quality and meaningful relationships with other members within the local church. We cannot grow and function effectively in vacillating isolation.

Within the local church, members must care for one another, suffer with one another, and rejoice with one another (see 1 Corinthians 12:21-26). To fail to care for one another is to cause division (see 1 Corinthians 12:25a). The body depends on its members caring for each other. God uses other human beings to provide for our needs (see Matthew 9:35-38, Luke 6:38, Romans 12:10). Believers have a basic need for a "sense of belonging" that can be met only in a small group. Therefore, the apostles brought members together in small groups (see Acts 2:46, 4:23-35, 20:20). Believers enjoyed a sociological unity as much as they enjoyed a theological unity (see Acts 2:44-46, 4:32). When our theology is correct and healthy, our sociology will also be correct and healthy (see Acts 7:22-26). When our sociology is unhealthy, our theology will also be unhealthy. Members must connect so that they will know how to exercise care.

A CULTURED CONTEXT WITHIN THE LOCAL CHURCH

The apostle Paul provided a context for the converts in Thessalonica. He introduced his converts to the notion of community, which proved to be very successful. People perform better within a cultured community context. Therefore, the church must become a context for its converts.

The church must provide an intellectual context within which converts can meditate (see 1 Thessalonians 1:5, 2:13). Believers must influence the thinking of elected politicians and appointed officials. The church must provide a social context within which converts can imitate (see 1 Thessalonians 1:6, 2:14-16). The church must provide an emotional context within which converts can recuperate (see 1 Thessalonians 2:17-20).

God designed the local church to meet all human needs. In his theory of the hierarchy of human needs, Abraham Maslow placed the need for self-actualization at the top. The church meets all our needs for self actualization (see Ephesians 3:20, Philippians 4:13). God wants His people to gather. The church is His gathering place for His people. We ought to place a premium on the Lord's church. Within the church, our needs are met. Therefore, we ought to praise God for meeting our needs with His church.

PURPOSE FOR THE LOCAL CHURCH

God designed the church to advance His ideas and ideals (see Ephesians 3:10). It must perpetuate the distinctive message that causes the church to come into existence. That message is that Jesus is both Lord and Christ (see Acts 2:36). As the Christ, Jesus is our redeemer. As Lord, Jesus is our ruler.

The church must also perpetuate the distinctive ministry that carries the church into its existence. This ministry consists of evangelism. Without evangelism, the church ceases to exist. Evangelism consists of a thorough indoctrination of what we possess in Christ, and a complete explanation of how we come to possess those spiritual possessions. Before we can evangelize, we must first be edified to grow in spiritual wisdom. Therefore, we gather for edification (see 1 Corinthians 14:5, 12, 26), but we scatter for evangelism (see Acts 8:4-5).

Disciples should participate within a local congregation because of their consideration for their own spiritual growth and development. Within the local congregation, each disciple receives instructions, fellowship, worship experiences, and discipline (see Acts 2:41-42, 20:7, 1 Corinthians 16:1-2, 2 Thessalonians 3:6-15).

The local church is a center for the testimony of the gospel (see 1 Thessalonians 1:8), a nursery for spiritual babies (see 1 Thessalonians

2:7-8), a family circle of prevailing love (see 1 Thessalonians 3:12), an environment of divine discipline (see 1 Thessalonians 4:6), a school of character instruction and development (see 1 Thessalonians 4:9-13), and a hospital for the spiritually weak (see 1 Thessalonians 5:14). Every disciple needs these benefits. Therefore, every disciple should participate within a local congregation.

God established the body of Christ universally for relationship (see Ephesians 2:11-16), but locally for function (see Acts 1:8, 2:1, 5, 6:7, 8:1-5, 12-14, 13:1-4, 14:1, 15:36). As family, we are all related to everyone, but we function with a few. The local church is God's gracious gathering for fellowship and function (see Acts 11:26, 1 Corinthians 11:33, Hebrews 10:24-25).

God authorized primary leaders for the body of Christ locally (see Acts 11:30, 14:23, Philippians 1:1-2, Titus 1:5). And He limited the jurisdiction of primary leaders to the believers among them locally (see 1 Peter 5:1-4). Primarily, God performs ministry through the body of Christ locally. We must lead according to a biblical model. The body of Christ locally is the most effective organism through which to do ministry, just as the local family is the most effective organism to raise children. Therefore we should pledge our allegiance to the body of Christ locally.

PROTECTION WITHIN THE LOCAL CHURCH

God protects us within the local church. The local church provides a layer of God's protection for us. Through our faithful fellowship within the local church, God provides a greater degree of protection for us. Therefore, satan has less power over those who remain within the fellowship of the local church. God provides a lesser degree of protection for those who are without the fellowship of the local church. Therefore, satan has more power over those who remain outside the fellowship of the local church.

A brother in the church at Corinth had an incestuous relationship with his father's wife (see 1 Corinthians 5:1, Leviticus 18:7-8). The apostle Paul recommended removing him from the fellowship of the church (see 1 Corinthians 5:2, 9-13). Removing him from the fellowship of the local church was equivalent to delivering him to satan (see 1 Corinthians 5:3-5a). Delivering him to satan resulted in the destruction of his flesh (see 1 Corinthians 5:5b). His destruction of the flesh took place outside the fellowship of the local church. The destruction of his flesh meant to (1) destroy his sinful nature so that he would repent, or (2) destroy his physical body if he refused to repent (see James 1:15).

When we fail to fellowship within the local church, we become more vulnerable to satanic attacks. Leaving the fellowship of the local church is a terribly dangerous thing to do. Keeping ourselves from the fellowship of the local church is suicidal. Keeping our children from the fellowship of the local church amounts to child abuse.

MEMBERSHIP WITHIN THE LOCAL CHURCH

Local church membership conforms to biblical concepts. The individualistic idea of "Jesus and only me" is foreign to scripture. God encounters mankind through covenant community. Becoming a member of the body of Christ universally was a separate and distinct issue from becoming a member of the body of Christ locally (see Acts 8:37-40). God ordained that each member of the body of Christ universally would become a faithful member of the body of Christ locally (see Hebrews 13:7, 17, 1 Thessalonians 5:12). Even now, God expects each member of the body of Christ universally to be accountable within the body of Christ locally. Let us consider accounts of acceptance into the body of Christ locally.

By devotion, members of the body of Christ universally became members of the body of Christ locally where they were baptized (see Acts 2:41-42). To be devoted is to remain faithfully in place (see Acts 1:14, 6:4, 8:13, 10:7). They devoted themselves to the apostles' doctrine, teaching and/or tutoring (see Titus 1:9). Doctrine originated with God (see Acts 2:4, John 14:26, 7:16). They devoted themselves to fellowship. To fellowship is to participate compatibly within a compatible activity because of compatible interests.

Believers became members of the body of Christ locally by *personal introduction* (see Acts 9:26-29). The apostle Paul, formerly known as Saul, had been baptized into the body of Christ universally (see Acts 9:1-18). Through baptism, God forgave him and washed away his sins (see Acts 22:16, 26:12-18). Immediately after becoming baptized into the body of Christ, he boldly preached the message of truth in Damascus (see Acts 9:20-22). Later, he went to Jerusalem. The disciples refused to receive him into the body of Christ at Jerusalem (see verse 26). Barnabas personally introduced Paul to the disciples at Jerusalem and they then welcomed him (see verses 27-28).

Believers became members of the body of Christ locally by *letter of recommendation* from those who were known to be faithful. Let us consider Phoebe (see Romans 16:1-16). She was a sister in Christ, a member of the body of Christ universally. Also, she was a servant in Cenchreae, a member of the body of Christ locally. The body of Christ existed in several localities (see verses 3-5, 16), but Phoebe was not a member at large, floating and drifting among them all. She had faithfully pledged her allegiance to the body of Christ at Cenchreae. Therefore by letter, the apostle Paul recommended her to the body of Christ at Rome.

Now, let us consider Apollos (see Acts 18:24-27). He was a learned preacher and a member of the body of Christ universally (see verses 24-26). Priscilla and Aquila taught him more accurately. Therefore, by letter the brethren recommended him to the body of Christ at Achaia (see verse 27). Also, we may consider John Mark (see Colossians 4:10). He was a faithful member of the body of Christ universally. Therefore, the apostle Paul wrote a letter to commend him to the body of Christ at church at Colossee.

Thought Provokers

1. Explain this statement: "The local church is a God idea."

2. What areas of your local fellowship are your serving in? Where else could you use the gifts that God has given you? Are there less-effective areas you would need to give up in order to be more effective?

3. Read 1 Corinthians 14:5, 12, 26, and Acts 8:4-5, then meditate on this statement: "We gather for edification but we scatter for evangelism." Where do you need to gather better? Where do you need to scatter better?

⁕ CHAPTER 12 ⁕

THE CHURCH OF GOD: THE MEMBERSHIP

MY GOD INTENDS FOR EACH MEMBER OF THE CHURCH to be strong and stable. As a result, we are no longer to be children, tossed here and there by waves and carried about by every wind of doctrine, by the trickery of men, by craftiness in deceitful scheming; but speaking the truth in love, we are to grow up in all aspects into Him who is the head, even Christ, from whom the whole body, being fitted and held together by what every joint supplies, according to the proper working of each individual part, causes the growth of the body for the building up of itself in love (Ephesians 4:14-16).

He knew that strong, stable church members would cause the church to grow. Therefore, He intended for each member to contribute to the growth of the church. In that regard, each member should be a leader. Some members should serve as primary leaders.

They are primary because God assigned their responsibilities. Initially, God assigned responsibilities to the apostles and prophets (see Ephesians 4:11). They served as the foundation of the church (see Ephesians 2:20). To these, God initially revealed His will (see Ephesians 3:1-5).

Subsequently, God assigned responsibilities to the evangelist and pastors/bishops/elders. Through His revelation to the apostles and prophets, God subsequently revealed His will to them. Yes, through His Word, God directly makes assignments to the evangelists (see 2 Timothy 4:1-5, 2:1-2, 14, 1 Timothy 6:17-19, Titus 2:15) and to the pastors/elders/bishops (see Acts 20:17-35, 1 Timothy 3:2-5, Titus 1:7-9).

While some members should serve as primary leaders, others should serve as secondary leaders. They are secondary because the primary leaders, not God, assigned their responsibilities. We call directly assigned leaders "primary leaders," and we call indirectly assigned leaders "secondary leaders." Primary leaders assign responsibilities to secondary leaders (specified, categorized, noticed) such as deacons, teachers, and ushers (see 2 Timothy 2:1-2, 1 Timothy 1:3). Scripture does not assign their responsibilities. Primary leaders assign responsibilities to secondary leaders (unspecified, uncategorized, unnoticed), such as who may be assigned to lock the building after services, or greet or call visitors.

There will always be more secondary leaders than primary leaders. Therefore, the greater amount of energy and potential lies within the realm of secondary leaders. Therefore, primary leaders are wise to tap into the energy and resources of the secondary. As a matter of fact, they must do so if the congregation is to be successful. Members can and will better support the ministry of the congregation when they are informed.

WHAT THE MEMBERSHIP SHOULD KNOW

We live in an information age wherein information abounds. Information gathering that once took weeks to accumulate can now be drawn together in seconds. The availability of information often whets the appetite for even more information. Members of the church are susceptible to this information influx as well. Likely, more and more members desire to know more and more about the church.

Members fall into at least four different categories. Some subscribe to the philosophy, "I have no need to know. I trust the leaders to do the right thing." Others say, "I have no need to know so that I can reduce conscience culpability just in case the leaders do not do the right thing." Still others say, "I need to know so that I can ensure that the leaders do the right thing." Yet others say, "I need to know so that I can better help the leaders do the right thing." Likely, many vacillate between these four categories, and end up with the eclectic blend that best fits their personality and personal preference.

During a casual conversation, I asked this question, "What should members know?" I discovered that members want to know church doctrine, church history, church membership requirements, church policy and procedure, the authority structure that establishes church policy and procedure, and holy living expectations. A more important question is, "What should members know per a perusal of scripture?"

This brings us to Acts chapter 6, which is the first biblical record of church conflict after the resurrection of Jesus. One day in the life of members provides a smorgasbord of information. Some disciples believed that their widows were being neglected (see verses 1-7). The apostles offered a solution that solved this dilemma. The solution to this problem led to church growth (see verse 7).

1. The members should know the congregation's priority emphasis. "Therefore, brethren, select from among you seven men of good reputation, full of the Spirit and of wisdom, whom we may put in charge of this task. But we will devote ourselves to prayer and to the ministry of the word" (verse 3-4). Neither the congregation nor any individual can do everything.

If we are a primary leader, what have we told the congregation about its priority emphasis? When a congregation has little or no knowledge of its priority emphasis, very little ministry will take place. If we are a secondary leader, what do we know about the congregation's priority emphasis? If we have heard, have we received, or are we resisting the priority emphasis?

2. The members should know that proclaiming the Word is the priority emphasis of the preaching servants. "Devote ourselves…to the ministry of the word" (verse 4). No doubt, those who believe that neglect had crept in wanted the care of the daily needs of widows to become more important to the whole congregation. The apostles quickly addressed this notion. The congregation and its leaders must decide how to communicate its priority.

The corporate world has coined the word *slippage.* Slippage is the daily, if not consciously monitored, tendency to replace the important with the urgent. It seems that Martha had replaced the important with the urgent (see Luke 10:41-42). Unless consciously monitored, the congregation will gradually wander away from the ministry of the Word. Has that happened where we worship? Is the ministry of the Word the priority emphasis? What percentage of our financial resources do we devote to a direct ministry of the Word? How much time and energy do we devote to a direct ministry of the Word? Does the congregation become more excited about participating in the ministry of the Word or about a potluck dinner?

3. The members should know that the preaching servants need to commune with God regularly in order to replenish themselves. "Devote ourselves to prayer" (Acts 6:4). Caretakers must take care of themselves. Those who invest in others must first invest in self so that they will have something to invest in others.

In my book *God, Listen! Prayers that God Always Answers,* I answer the question, "What does God do when we pray?" Interestingly, God gives courage and power. What ministry servant can serve effectively without courage and power? Therefore, God does through us what we can do, and He does for us what we cannot do. In this same book, I also answer the question, "What does prayer do when we pray?" Prayer brings us into a conscious awareness of God and into a consulting alliance with God. How much more effectively can ministry servants minister the Word when they have conscious awareness of God and are operating within a consulting alliance with God? We can readily understand why the apostles placed prayer within the priority paradigm of their personal lifestyle.

4. The members should know that a division of ministry responsibilities does exist. "It is not desirable for us to neglect the word of God in order to serve tables" (Acts 6:2). There needs to be a division of responsibilities within the congregation. Jesus succeeded as a leader. He organized well (see Luke 9:14, 10:1, Acts 1:8). The workforce must be organized according to capability and availability. The workload must be organized according to what is important and what is urgent.

5. The members should know which ministry servants will not do what. "It is not desirable for us" (Acts 6:2).

6. The members should know which ministry servants will do what: "whom we may put in charge of this task" (verse 3).

7. The members need to know that the jurisdiction of each secondary ministry leader and/or servant is limited to his assigned area of responsibility: "in charge of this task" (verse 3).

8. The members need to know when additional ministry servants will be added: "So the twelve summoned the congregation of the disciples" (verse 2).

9. The members need to know how many personnel resources are needed: "seven men" (verse 3).

10. The members need to know the character quality of its ministry servants: "of good reputation, full of the Spirit and of wisdom" (verse 3).

11. The members need to know who the ministry servants are: "Stephen, a man full of faith and of the Holy Spirit, and Philip,

Prochorus, Nicanor, Timon, Parmenas and Nicolas, a proselyte from Antioch" (verse 5).

12. The members need to know when ministry servants have been selected: "They laid their hands on them" (verse 6).

What should the membership know? The membership should know as much as necessary to enhance the growth of the church. Knowledge beyond what enhances the spiritual stamina and vibrancy of the church is unnecessary.

Each disciple of Christ is interdependent of each other disciple (see 1 Corinthians 12:21-26). We all need each other. The eye is hampered in functioning if it assumes that the hand is unnecessary. It may spot the food, but cannot pick it up (see verse 21). In this spiritual web of relationships, a support group emerges that ought to care for the weak, the less honorable, and the unseemly (see verse 26). The Christian life is relationships with others, not an isolated experience.

Thought Provokers

1. How has your understanding of God's church changed as a result of reading this chapter?

2. Would you consider yourself a primary or secondary leader in your local fellowship? How did you come to that conclusion?

3. As a result of your assessment of your leadership position, what are your roles within your local fellowship, and where might you need to change what you are doing?

◈ CHAPTER 13 ◈

THE WILL OF GOD

MY GOD PLACED HIS "GOOD" STAMP OF APPROVAL UPON the whole of creation. "God saw all that He had made, and behold, it was very good. And there was evening and there was morning, the sixth day" (Genesis 1:31). Although God called it "good," we must admit that for quite sometime, agonizing turmoil has existed within the human head, heart, and hand. Elemental turmoil in the earth (volcanic eruptions), on the earth (floods), and above the earth (atmospheric storms) has caused much pain and suffering. These tragedies bring forth many questions relative to the "will of God."

THE CURSE

Sin ushered in a curse upon the whole of creation. A curse was a divine sentence of punishment that restricted and/or removed from someone or something the potential power to perform for good. The curse of the fig tree removed its potential power ever to produce (good) figs (see Mark 11:12-14, 20-21). Because of sin, God cursed the creation (see Genesis 3:13-19, 5:29, 8:21). The curse restricted and in some cases removed from the whole of creation its potential power to perform for good.

Sin brought about the curse of the flood (see Genesis 2:5-6, 6:5, 11-13, 7:4, 12). The curse of the flood brought about a catastrophic deterioration within the universe. It changed seedtime, harvest, cold, heat, summer, winter, day, and night (see Genesis 7:21-23, 8:1-2, 21-22). Immediately after the flood, the length of human life significantly declined (see Genesis 5:27, 11:10-32, 23:1, 25:17). Very likely, the curse of the flood restricted and in some cases even removed some of the human body's rejuvenating potential. Indeed, all problems within humanity—physical, spiritual, moral, social, political, and economical—can be traced to the curse. All problems within the elements can be traced to the curse. Even now, the sin-curse principle is still operating within the universe, restricting and removing potential for good. The apostle Paul described how "the whole creation groans and suffers the pains of childbirth together until now" (Romans 8:22).

The sin-curse brought death (see Genesis 2:15-17). All have sinned (see Romans 3:23). Therefore, the question is not, "Why does God allow anyone to die?" but, "Why does God allow anyone to live?" Now that is grace and mercy.

Have we a lease on life? May we not also soon vanish away? Should we not immediately heed His warning? We are all flood victims. We have not witnessed the last human upheaval in nature, nor have we witnessed the last sin-caused crime. In spite of it all, we ought to trust God, applaud Jesus, and anticipate eternal life. God will ultimately reverse the Edenic curse (see Revelation 22:1-3). Therefore, we should be looking for a new Heaven and a new Earth wherein righteousness dwells (see 2 Peter 3:10-13). Our hope is the resurrection.

PERCEPTION OF GOD

What is our perception of God? From where did our perception come? Did we obtain most of our perception by listening to God or just talking to ourselves?

God withheld some knowledge from the prophets and even the angels (see 1 Peter 1:10-12, Ephesians 3:5). The knowledge that He once withheld, He later revealed through Jesus Christ (see Ephesians 3:1-6). Yes, God withheld the full revelation of Himself until the coming of Jesus Christ.

Within the Old Testament, God only partially revealed Himself. He anticipated His full revelation that was to come through Jesus Christ. Therefore, we must interpret God and His will before the coming of Christ in light of everything we learn about God and His will after the coming of Christ. Through Jesus Christ, God provides the most comprehensive portrait of Himself. What do we learn about God by looking at Jesus Christ?

Jesus is the living logo of God (see John 1:1-3, 14). The word *Word* was translated from the Greek word *logos*. It has been transliterated into the English language as *logo*. A logo is a visible representation and demonstration of a concept. Jesus is the visible representation and demonstration of the concept of God. Jesus visibly represents and demonstrates the concept of God (see John 14:6-11).

Jesus is the image icon of God (see Colossians 1:15-20). The word *image* comes from the Greek word *eikon*. It has been translated into the English language as *icon*. An icon is a self-interpreting identity. Jesus is the self-interpreting identity of God. Jesus is the clearest identity picture of God (see Hebrews 1:1-3). Therefore, our mental picture of God determines our attitude toward God. Our attitude toward God dictates our actions toward God. Any mental picture of God that is inconsistent with the biblical picture of Jesus is the wrong picture of God. Any mental picture of God that fails to draw us to Jesus is the wrong picture of God (see John 6:44).

Evil in general exists because angels and/or human beings rejected and even now are rejecting the will of God. A vast matrix of interlocking freedom choices of human beings and/or angels accounted for many outcomes. Satan, Judas, Roman officials, chief priests, Pharisees, Annas, Caiaphas, Pilate, Herod, and the multitude corroborated to crucify Jesus (see John 13:26-27, 18:3, 12-13, 28-40, 19:1-16). It is beyond human comprehension to determine the determinant cause of every instance of evil.

The will of God is a determining factor of outcomes within the universe, but what really is the will of God? God has an ideal will: that which He prefers. God prefers sinlessness. "My little children, *I am writing these things to you so that you may not sin*. And if anyone sins, we have an Advocate with the Father, Jesus Christ the righteous" (1 John 2:1 emphasis added).

God has a circumstantial will: that which He permits. Although God prefers sinlessness, He permits sinfulness (see 1 John 2:1b, 1:9-10). God preferred that Adam and Eve not eat of the fruit of the tree of knowledge of good and evil (see Genesis 2:16-17), yet He permitted them to eat (see Genesis 3:6). God preferred that human beings live forever (see Genesis 3:22-23), yet He permitted them to die (see Genesis 3:24). God preferred that there would be no divorce (see 1 Corinthians 7:10), yet He permitted divorce (see verse 11a). After permitting divorce, He prefers reconciliation (see verse 11b).

God's circumstantial will is where we are. God's ideal will is where we fell from, yet where He still helps us to be. God's grace moves us from where we are to where He wants us to be. In Jesus, God has made us perfect and holy.

Through caring persuasion, God seeks to move us from His circumstantial will (that which He permits) toward His ideal will (that which He prefers). God does not always govern us through coercive domination, however. The words and the works of Jesus were always perfectly consistent with the words and works of God, His Father (see John 14:10). His words were the very works of God. Jesus always positioned Himself perfectly within the will of His Father. Therefore, the will of God is found wherever Jesus is found.

WHERE DOES JESUS POSITION HIMSELF?

Jesus positions Himself on the side with good health (see Luke 4:38-41). Therefore, poor health is inconsistent with the ideal will of God.

We should pay no attention to statements that suggest that God put us on our back so that we would look up to Him.

Jesus positions Himself on the side with a successful fishing expedition (see Luke 5:1-6). Therefore, successful business ventures are consistent with the ideal will of God. We should pay no attention to those who suggest that God caused our business to fail.

Jesus positions Himself in opposition to spiritual and intellectual illiteracy (see Luke 6:20-49). Therefore, being present to receive instructions is consistent with the ideal will of God. We should pay no attention to those who say, "I will come to class if it is God's will."

Jesus positions Himself on the side with freedom from leprosy (see Luke 5:12-15). Therefore, freedom from contagious diseases is consistent with the ideal will of God. We should pay no attention to those who say that God put sickness upon us to teach us a lesson. What a way to teach a lesson that most would never learn, even though they may have been ill for years. Surely, God must have a more productive teaching method.

Jesus positions Himself on the side with forgiveness from sin (see Luke 5:20). Therefore, forgiveness of sin is consistent with the ideal will of God. We should pay no attention to those who say that God caused sin to come upon us. Jesus came to take away sin. Do not call a blessing what God calls sin.

Jesus positions Himself on the opposing side from paralysis (see Luke 5:21-26). Therefore, movable joints and freedom from arthritis are consistent with the ideal will of God.

Jesus positions Himself on the opposing side from troubling unclean spirits (see Luke 6:17-19). Therefore, freedom from mental oppression is consistent with the ideal of God.

The will of God is found wherever Jesus is found. God wants us to interpret Him through His portrait of Jesus, for through Jesus, God provided the most comprehensive portrait of Himself. Through Him, God has demonstrated the fullness of His love for humanity (see 1 John 3:1, 16).

WHAT HAPPENED?

The lie about God is the foundation for the downward drift of humanity. The belief of the lie started our downward drift. Eve believed the lie that God had withheld something good from her (see Genesis 3:4-6). The belief of the lie continues our downward drift (see Romans 1:18-25).

The truth about Jesus is the foundation for the upward trend of humanity. The belief of the truth started our upward trend (see Genesis 3:15). The belief of the truth continues our upward trend (see Acts 8:5-14). Therefore, we must consciously combat each specific lie about God with a specific truth about God from the Word of God.

Many ask, "Why doesn't God do something?" God created the world. He interacted with His created world. He interacted with His created world in accordance with His design purpose for the creation. Understanding God's design purpose for His creation will better help us to understand God's interaction with His creation. What was God's purpose in the creation?

God is love (see 1 John 4:8-16). The creation is all about the love of God. God created the world that He might extend His love (1) downward to people, from Him to us (see Romans 5:5, 1 John 3:1, 4:7b), (2) upward to Him, from us to Him (see 1 John 4:19-5:2), and (3) outward to others, from us to others (see 1 John 3:11, 23, 4:7a, 11).

The love of God was His attitude and action caused by our need, but regulated by His relationship and resources. We needed salvation; therefore, through Jesus, God satisfied our sin debt (see 1 John 4:9-10). Through Jesus, God demonstrated the fullest extent of His love. God is love all the time. We consistently see the love of God within His provisions. We see the love of God within His tangible provisions (see Genesis 1:29, 2:7-9). We see the love of God within His intangible provisions (see Genesis 1:26-28). We can consistently see the love of God within His prohibitions. Just as with children, immaturity keeps us from seeing the love that lies within prohibitions. Love within His prohibitions helps us to avoid intrinsic penalties and the pain of guilt and brokenness (see Genesis 2:15-18, 3:6-11). The love within His prohibitions also helps us to avoid instrumental penalties, occasionally immediate death and ultimately eternal death (see Genesis 3:17-24).

Our love for God should cause us to resist the temptation to supersede God—that is, to become all knowing (see verse 5). When we try to seize what properly belongs to God (all knowledge, and judgment), we lose what properly belongs to us (life) (see verse 22). If our attitude toward God fails to inspire passionate service through Jesus Christ, we have the wrong image of God. Both mature and immature may see love in provisions, but only the mature see love in the prohibitions. Therefore, we should express our appreciation as much for God's prohibitions as we do for His provisions.

Understanding God's design purpose for His creation will better help us to understand God's interaction with His creation. God interacts with His creation in such a way that extends His love downward to humanity. Therefore, God is not the originator of any activity that interferes with His love flowing downward. God interacts with His creation in such a way that extends His love upward to Himself. Therefore, God is not the originator of any activity that interferes with His love flowing upward. God interacts with His creation in such a way that extends His love outward to others. Therefore, God is not the originator of any activity that interferes with His love flowing outward.

God interacts with His creation in such a way to enable man to speak good words. Therefore, God is not the originator of any activity that interferes with good words being spoken. God interacts with His creation in such a way to enable man to perform good works. Therefore, God is not the originator of any activity that interferes with good works being done. Give all activity the love test. Unless it passes the love test, do not charge it to God.

God is glory (see 2 Peter 1:16-17, Hebrews 1:3). The creation is all about the glory of God. He created the world that He might extend His glory. Since God created man in His own image and likeness, man is to be the crowning glory of the love of God's creation. God orchestrated the entire creation to share His love for man and to share His glory with man. Yes, God created man to share in His glory (see John 17:1-5, 20-22).

Understanding God's design purpose for His creation will better help us to understand God's interaction with His creation. God interacts with His creation in such a way to enable man to be seen as His crowning glory. Therefore, God is not the originator of any activity that interferes with man being seen as the crowning glory of God. Give all activity the glory test. Unless it passes the glory test, do not charge it to God. It is not according to the ideal will of God.

Revelation chapters 6-22 give us a picture of what has and will happen to God's creation. The seven seals indicate that the world had been ruined by man (see Revelation 5:1-5). The seven trumpets indicate that the world was ruled by satan (see Revelation 8:2-6). The seven bowls, however, indicate that the world would be rescued by God (see Revelation 16:1, 17:1, 21:9). Therefore, the next time we wonder, "Why doesn't God do something?" we should remember that God *is* doing something. Through caring persuasion, not coercive domination, He is working according to His will. His will is in accordance with His design purpose for the creation.

God created the world to extend His love and glory. He extends His love and glory through caring persuasion, not through coercive domination (see Luke 13:34). Caring persuasion allows for freedom to choose. Freedom to choose allows for the probability of the rejection of God. Rejection of God injects evil into the world (see Genesis 3:6, Genesis 4:7, Romans 5:12, 1 John 3:12).

God created angels (see Colossians 1:16). and gave them the freedom to choose. He created human beings and gave them freedom to choose (see Deuteronomy 30:15-20). The nature of the creation itself allows for the possibility of evil. Some angels rejected God (see 2 Peter 2:4, Jude 6). Some human beings rejected God (see Genesis 3:6, Romans 1:18-32). Rejection by angels and/or human beings promotes and perpetuates evil within the world (see James 4:17, 1 John 3:4).

God is all powerful, yet He does not exercise all power in making angels nor people obey. God chooses to operate within the universe through caring persuasion. The will of God is a determining factor of outcomes within the universe. Opposition to the will of God (see rebelling angels and/or rebelling human beings) is also a determining factor of outcomes within the universe. Therefore, everything that happens within the universe is not according to the will of God (see John 12:31, 2 Corinthians 4:3-4, 1 John 3:8).

Why does evil in general exist? In general, evil exists because angels and/or human beings reject the will of God. The created design of freedom of choice allows for the possibility of evil to exist. Why does evil in specific exist? A vast matrix of interlocking freedom choices among human beings and/or angels account for many outcomes (see John 13:26-27, 18:3, 12-13, 28-40 19:1-16). Therefore it is beyond human comprehension to determine the determinant cause of every instance of evil.

The devil opposes a healthy spirit, soul, and body. God favors a healthy spirit, soul, and body. Therefore, through Jesus Christ, God opposes the devil (see 1 John 3:8). Deformity is not according to a meticulous plan of God (see Luke 13:11-17). The spirit of satan bound this woman in her deformity (see Luke 13:11, 16). The spirit of the Savior released the woman from her deformity (see verses 12-13).

Oppression is not according to a meticulous plan of God (see Luke 4:14-20). Luke summarized the ministry of Jesus as one that does good. "You know of Jesus of Nazareth, how God anointed Him with the Holy Spirit and with power, and how He went about doing good and healing all who were oppressed by the devil, for God was with Him" (Acts 10:38). The spirit of satan produced oppression, while the spirit of the Savior released from oppression.

The will of God is a determining factor of outcomes within the universe. Opposition to the will of God is a determining factor of outcomes within the universe. There is not a specific divine reason for everything that happens. The ultimate reason why things happen is not that God decided it was better to have it happen than not to have it happen. Everything that happens is not according to the ideal will of God. And in any event, God does not have to justify to us why some live and some die (see Luke 13:3-5).

My God—has He stimulated your thought? He should stimulate thought and further thought. He will challenge your thoughts and challenge you to think. For some, this book may have been too elementary to stimulate much thought, but for others, it may be challenging. In either case, I invite you to give it another try. Go ahead. Give it a try. Read it again. Then read it again.

My God should help you to see and believe that God wants you to consider Him as your friend. Study His kindness and gentleness, and seek to pattern after them. Even through His awesomeness, God remains personable.

My God should help you to appreciate and appropriate Him as He has revealed Himself within His Word. You will get to know Him. After all, He is easy to get to know for He has made Himself available. "The Lord is with you when you are with Him. And if you seek Him, He will let you find Him" (2 Chronicles 15:2).

My God should help you to admire His reputation even while you see His authority. Seeing Him clearly should therefore clear up many misconceptions you may have about the will of God for your life. My God should help you to correct your perspective of God. Therefore, while you are pondering the very concept of God, take another look at Him through His creative lenses. Although you may read this book in a matter of hours, do spend the rest of your life viewing God through the portrait of His Son. You will never be bored, nor will you ever exhaust the depth nor height nor breadth of His magnificence. He is my God. He is your God.

FOR THE RECORD

Within Scripture, a distinct organism called the church existed. *Before* the death, burial, and resurrection, of Jesus Christ, Scripture declared that the church *would* come into existence (see Matthew 16:17-18). *After* the death, burial, and resurrection of Jesus Christ, Scripture declared that the church had *already* come into existence (see Acts 8:1-3).

The preaching of the death, burial, and resurrection of Jesus Christ resulted in people becoming forgiven of sins (see Acts 2:36-38). The preaching of the death, burial, and resurrection of Jesus Christ resulted in people becoming saved (see Acts 2:47). The preaching of the death, burial, and resurrection of Jesus Christ resulted in people becoming members of the church (see Acts 2:47).

Becoming forgiven of sins is equivalent to becoming saved, which is equivalent to becoming a member of the church. Those who are forgiven have become saved. Those who are saved are members of the church. One cannot become a member of the church without becoming saved. One cannot become saved without becoming a member of the church. So, to be saved is to be in the church, and to be in the church is the same as being saved.

The church, the body of Christ, came to exist only after the resurrection of Jesus. Christianity rises and/or falls on the resurrection of Jesus. The resurrection is more than a contemporary Easter idea; it is the very essence of Christianity. Christians pledge themselves not to a festive holiday program, but to a person, the resurrected Lord Jesus Christ.

The message of the death, burial, and resurrection of Jesus brought the church into existence. An appropriate response of faith toward the death, burial, and resurrection of Jesus brings a person into a forgiven state, saved, and into the church.

Believing that Jesus is the Christ, the Son of God, is an adequate response of faith. The death, burial, and resurrection of Jesus proves that He is the Christ, the Son of God (see Romans 1:1-4, Acts 17:30-31). Therefore, only those who believe can become forgiven of sins, saved, and members of the church (see John 8:24, Acts 4:1-4, 8:35-37).

Repenting of sin is an adequate response of faith. Repentance is the change of heart within a person (see Matthew 21:28-32). In repentance, you change your allegiance (see Acts 2:38, 17:30, 26:19-20). You remove your allegiance to your selfish self and pledge your allegiance to the Savior.

Becoming baptized is an adequate response of faith. Baptism is your response to the call of God (see 1 Peter 3:21). Near the beginning of his ministry, the apostle Peter preached about baptism. Near the end of his ministry, the apostle

Peter wrote about baptism. Even now baptism saves. What is baptism?

First, we consider the dry side of baptism. It is a response of the mind, for it is an internal appeal toward God. The dry side is a response of the conscience. The conscience is a product of accepted teachings (see John 8:1-9, Leviticus 20:10). The dry side is a response of a *good* conscience. Within this context, a good conscience is a heart that trusts in the resurrection of Jesus Christ (see 1 Peter 3:21). The resurrection proves that Jesus is the son of God (see Romans 1:4, Acts 17:31). Only those who believe in the resurrection of Jesus have a good conscience for baptism (see John 8:24, Acts 8:35-37). If your conscience is insufficiently taught, your conscience will be insufficiently developed. And if your conscience is incorrectly taught, then it will be incorrectly developed.

Baptism takes place while the penitent believer is in water (see Acts 8:36-39). Baptism consists of taking the penitent believer to the water, and never bringing the water to the penitent believer. We should never attempt to reduce baptism to sprinkling and pouring of water. Some object to the necessity of being covered in water, but Jesus was sealed in His tomb (see Matthew 27:62-64, Romans 6:4). Some object to the necessity of water, yet water is specifically mentioned (see Acts 8:36-39, 10:47, 1 Peter 3:20-21). God refused to heal Naaman until he went into the water (see 2 Kings 5:14).

When those who heard the gospel believed, repented, and became baptized, they were forgiven, saved, and became a member of the church. Even now, a faith response to the death, burial, and resurrection of Jesus Christ allows one to become forgiven of sins, saved, and a Christian.

How much must one know before becoming baptized? I favor teaching an abundance of truth, yet we must ask, how much does the Scripture indicate that believers knew before they became baptized? How can we know how much a person knows? We know how much a person knows only by how much they indicate that they know. How much did early believers indicate they knew before being baptized? They indicated only that they believed that Jesus was the son of God (see Acts 8:37).

Believers need to know how to worship, where to worship, the nature of the church, and how to behave as a Christian, yet early believers were never called upon to demonstrate that level of knowledge prior to becoming baptized. Saying that one has become a Christian differs from saying that one has learned how to behave as a Christian (see Matthew 28:18-20). Some have become Christians, yet are worshipping in error. We must call them out of all religious error.

Who can baptize? The status of the one who teaches and baptizes has no effect upon the resulting state of the penitent believer. If it did, believers would be held responsible for what they could not possibly know, for no person can really know the heart of another.

Where must one be baptized? One can be baptized any place there is adequate water for a burial. Remember that only those who have believed, repented, and become baptized have become forgiven of sins, saved, and a member of the church. Nevertheless, all those who have believed, repented, and become baptized have become forgiven of sins, saved, and a member of the church.

Why is there so much confusion on subject of baptism? An intellectual exegesis of Scripture (bringing out of the text the ideas of the author) rather than an emotional exegesis of Scripture (bringing into the text the ideas of the reader) peels away most of the layers of confusion. The Holy Spirit could not come until after Jesus had risen from the dead and ascended to Heaven (see John 16:7). Some forty days after Jesus had risen from the dead, the Holy Spirit was yet to come (see Acts 1:1-8). The Holy Spirit came on the day of Pentecost (see Acts 2:1-4). The Holy Spirit revealed the message of truth to those who wrote Scripture (see Ephesians 3:1-5, 2 Peter 1:21). The apostle Peter spoke the words of Acts 2:38 before Matthew, Mark, Luke, and John wrote the words contained in their gospels. Being from regions beyond Jerusalem, most of those who heard the words of Acts 2:38 had not heard Jesus speak (see Acts 2:9-11). Even those who had heard Jesus speak failed to understand His message; therefore they crucified Him (see Acts 3:17, 1 Corinthians 2:8).

Historically, the Jews offered sacrifices with an understanding that they would invoke the forgiveness (appeasement) of God. Even on Pentecost, they believed that they needed to respond in order to receive forgiveness of God. Therefore, they asked, "What shall we do?" (see Acts 2:37). Peter had just preached a persuasive sermon designed to convince the audience that Jesus was the Christ and Lord (see Acts 2:36). Obviously, some who heard also believed, for their hearts were pricked (see Acts 2:37). Hearts are never pricked until belief comes. In addition to believing, they asked what to do. In other words, they were now asking, "After believing, what (else) shall we do?"

If they had been forgiven (saved) just by believing, Peter should have told them so. If they had been saved just by believing, Peter misled them by allowing them to believe that there was something they needed to do in order to be saved. In the past, they had killed and offered an animal in their effort to receive forgiveness of sins. Peter informed them that no longer would they have to kill a lamb. The lamb (Jesus) had already been slain. Now, they must repent and be baptized to embrace the death of Jesus. Only after Jesus had been raised from the dead did He make the connection or correlate baptism with salvation (see Mark 16:16). No wonder then that Peter relates baptism to salvation (see Acts 2:38).

But what about Romans 10:9-10? Let's set the stage.

1. Those to whom the apostle Paul addressed this letter were called and had become saints (see Romans 1:6-7).
2. They had died to sin (see Romans 6:2).
3. They had been baptized into Christ and His death (see Romans 6:3).
4. They had been raised from the dead to walk in the newness of life (see Romans 6:4).

5. They had become united with Jesus (see Romans 6:5).
6. Their old self had been crucified with Christ (see Romans 6:6).
7. They had obeyed from the heart the doctrinal teachings (see Romans 6:17).
8. They had been freed from sin (see Romans 6:18).
9. They had become servants of righteousness (see Romans 6:18).
10. Jews from Rome had been in Jerusalem on Pentecost (see Acts 2:10). It is likely they were baptized at that time.

Therefore, the apostle Paul said to the believers—those who had already been baptized—"Confess and believe" (see Romans 10:9-10).

What about Ephesians 2:8, which states, "For by grace you have been saved through faith"? The Ephesians had heard the message of truth (see Ephesians 1:13a). They had believed the message of truth (see Ephesians 1:13b). They had been baptized (see Acts 19:1-5). In Acts 8:30-32, the eunuch did not understand what he was reading from Isaiah chapter 53. Philip began at Isaiah 53:7, the place where the eunuch was reading, and preached Jesus to him (see Acts 8:35).

1. How could Philip preach Jesus when the name Jesus is not once stated in Isaiah chapter 53?
2. How could Philip demand that the eunuch believe that Jesus Christ is the Son of God when believing that Jesus Christ is the Son of God is never stated in Isaiah chapter 53?

3. How could Philip introduce the subject of baptism while preaching Jesus from Isaiah chapter 53 when baptism is not stated in Isaiah chapter 53?

4. How did Philip understand Isaiah chapter 53 when the eunuch did not?

The answers to all four questions are the same. Philip had a Holy Spirit-led post-resurrection understanding of the Old Testament (see Acts 6:5) and the eunuch did not. God more fully revealed His will to the apostles and prophets (see Ephesians 3:5). Philip had heard the message from the apostles in Jerusalem (see Acts 6:1-5). There are some things that had not been understood before, but came to be understood only after the resurrection of Jesus.

Because Philip had a Holy Spirit-led post-resurrection understanding of the Old Testament, God enlightened him to understand things more fully than others understood. God enlightened His apostles and prophets to understand the Old Testament. When we read the New Testament, we gain insight into the inspired minds of the apostles and prophets (see Ephesians 3:5). Jesus recognized that men needed a post-resurrection understanding of the Old Testament scriptures. Therefore, He opened their minds to understand them (see Luke 24:44-47). God opened Lydia's mind to understand (see Acts 16:14); her understanding led her to be baptized (see Acts 16:15). The Corinthians had been baptized (see Acts 18:8). Earlier, Paul alluded to their baptism (see 1 Corinthians 6:8-11). He even reminded them of the role of baptism in the deliverance of the Israelites (see 1 Corinthians 10:1-4).

Where does the Old Testament teach the purpose of baptism? It does not. It just illustrates it. The lamb's blood became available for the Israelites (see Exodus 12:21-28), yet the Israelites were not free from bondage until they passed through the sea (see Exodus 14:26-29). God saved Israel on the day that they passed through the water (see Exodus 14:30). The Holy Spirit's inspired commentary called that experience a baptism:

> For I do not want you to be unaware, brethren, that our fathers were all under the cloud, and all passed through the sea; and all were baptized into Moses in the cloud and in the sea; and all ate the same spiritual food; and all drank the same spiritual drink, for they were drinking from a spiritual rock which followed them; and the rock was Christ (1 Corinthians 10:1-4).

Scripture does provide a roadmap toward the salvation that is found only in Christ Jesus. We can ascertain the will of God through reading Scripture. Obedience to this guidance results in the best possible life on earth as well as positions us for the best possible life beyond this earth.

OTHER BOOKS BY JOHN MARSHALL

Good and Angry
A Personal Guide to Anger Management

God, Listen!
Prayers That God Always Answers
(includes addiction-recovery guide)

The Power of the Tongue
What You Say Is What You Get

Final Answer:
You Asked, God Answered

Success Is a God Idea

Show Me the Money
7 Exercises That Build Economic Strength

God Knows!
There Is No Need to Worry

FOR MORE INFORMATION

For further information about John Marshall, his ministry, and his ministry resources, please contact him at:

JC   John Davis Marshall
PO Box 2136
Stone Mountain GA 30086
(404) 297-9050   jdm@graceview.us
www.graceview.us
www.graceview.us
jdm@graceview.us